My Life Before During and After Elvis Presley

By John Wilkinson
&
Nick Moretti

Table of Contents

Introduction 5
John's Acknowledgements 13
Nick's Acknowledgements 17
Forward 19
Prologue 23
Earliest Memories 31
Growing Up Music 43
The Horizon of Music Expands 51
Rock and Roll Radio Days 59
Discovered 77
Rainy Day Friends 87
Recording for RCA and the Late 1960s 101
All the King's Men 113
Taking Care of Business 135
My Friend, Elvis 155
The Touring Years 167
Aloha, People of Earth! 183
Known Only to Him 207
Performing for the Fans 217
TCB Reunion 233

Introduction by Peter Verbruggen

IT WAS APRIL, 1992. Kaiserslautern, Germany. I was barely 25 years old and my childhood dream was about to come true. Promoter Jacques Delessert had invited me to attend the "Elvis Show" in the Barbarossa Halle in his hometown.

I was a journalist at the time (still am), and somehow I had managed to convince my boss to let me do a full-page report on this "spectacular show." I did cheat a bit and told him that there would be at least 5,000 people—while in reality only 1,200 tickets were sold. But who cares, right? I was on my way to my very first Elvis Tribute Show!

On stage would be: JD Sumner and the Stamps, the Jordanaires, Sean Nielsen, Kathy Westmoreland and … John Wilkinson. All my heroes. I mean growing up with Elvis's music, I knew all these names but not the people behind the names.

Going to Kaiserslautern was a big thrill for me. First off, it was my very first "international" report but second, I got an invitation to meet the band on Friday evening, during the pre-show party in a beautiful old castle. Meeting JD, Kathy… needless to say that I was in seventh heaven. After all, these were the people that worked with Elvis on stage. The guy with no sleeves in his shirt … the little girl with the beautiful high voice … JD, who let Elvis in through the back door in the '50s and became Elvis's confidant and second father … and of course, John Wilkinson.

You have to know, right at the end of my bed hung a poster that I had brought with me from Italy. It showed Elvis in 1975 and, next to him, his loyal and always-present rhythm guitar player. For more than 10 years, the last thing I saw before I turned out the light, was John. And the first thing I saw when the alarm clock went off ... was John. Now, April 1992, this same man was in Europe. I knew that he had suffered a stroke (April, 1989) but I was desperate to meet him. Elvis Presley's guitarist! How much closer can you get to the real thing?

When I walked in the central hall of the old castle, I spotted John right away. Much to my surprise, he was sitting there all by himself, drinking a coke, enjoying a little cigarillo. If I remember well, Sean and the Jordanaires were singing around a piano, Kathy had already gone to bed, and JD was doing an interview for local television. I waited, and waited ... Should I go up to John? Or wait until he looked our way? How would he react? Would he understand my English? Would he have time for me? Would he even be interested?

At that time, I had done interviews with several music celebrities; John Hiatt, Garth Brooks and Mike Stipe (REM) among them. But none of these guys had played with Elvis. So in short, I walked up to John, introduced myself and told him that I was a journalist for a Belgian newspaper.

I don't know if it's ever happened to you but when John answered me there was this magical spark that said, "It's OK, I'm your friend." Was it the tone of his voice, his friendly reply, his soft eyes? I can't say, but I felt at ease right away.

"An interview? Sure, have a seat."

What I experienced so many times later was a real discovery that evening. John has a very special gift: He touches people, makes them comfortable. It's almost as if you're talking in your own language to somebody who understands you 100 percent. The ice was broken and John agreed to do an interview the next morning at 10 a.m. in the breakfast bar. Knowing that I had talked to John Wilkinson and that we would do an interview, I went to bed happily. Well, "bed" may not be the right word. All the rooms in the castle were booked and all they found for me was a mattress in the sauna. But hey, that's OK. I knew that this weekend would change my life forever.

The following morning, 10 on the dot, John was waiting for me at the breakfast bar. I still have that interview; I taped it with an old cassette recorder ... and I still listen to it once in awhile. It doesn't take long to hear the love for Elvis in John's voice. He talks with respect, friendship and admiration about his former boss and friend. Never a harsh word. Several stories on that tape go into detail: about how he learned about Elvis's death, his first meeting with the King, those strange concerts at the giant Houston Astrodome ("The acoustics are so bad, that if you finish a song, it comes right back at ya"), the bitter cold New Years's Eve show in 1976 ("I thought of playing with my gloves on") and of course the first Vegas Show in July of 1969 ("It was like grabbing an electrical wire"). I guess we talked for more than an hour or so, until somebody came up to our table and asked John if he could come with him for a sound check.

We had our picture taken—still my favourite to this day—and said good-bye. Well, not good-bye actually, it was "so long!" And I remember clearly, I said, "One day, John, sooner or later, I'll invite you to my home country, Belgium."

Now there I was: I talked to the man whose picture dominated my room and I promised him to invite him over to Belgium.

When I came home, I sent John a long letter, including some pictures and a copy of my newspaper. It said: "The highlight of the show was, indisputably, the performance of John Wilkinson." I was a fan. Of Elvis, and now of his guitarist too.

Over the years (and this was before the e-mail and Internet revolution), we stayed in touch. He wrote me letters, sent me faxes ... and I still have all of them! I remember sending John a bootleg CD that I found at a record fair. It was recorded in Lake Tahoe, 1976, and featured John Wilkinson playing and singing "Early Morning Rain," his signature song in the '70s. John was thrilled to death. He knew that he had sung the song several times onstage when Elvis held the mic for him but he had never really heard it. And now, with the booming market for unofficial Elvis CDs, there was the song! And wouldn't you know, a few days later I got a big brown envelope in the mail, from John. In it was a beautiful Celtic cross and a handwritten letter:

"This is the cross that I wore on opening night in Vegas, 1969. Before we went onstage, Elvis came over to me and clutched the cross in his hands and said, 'I'm glad you're here John'."

This Celtic cross is still—by far—one of my most prized possessions. It meant the world to me.

And then, finally in 1998, I sent John a fax that, in a way, would change his life too. I had finished writing a book called, "Elvis – King of Belgium," about the rise of Elvis Presley in a country he never even visited. John wrote the preface and for its official presentation at the Cultural Center in Mol, I needed a special guest. Who else but John? My friend Sis, in charge of the bookings for the Cultural Center at the time, suggested to book a live band too. So Geert Vanlommel, a very talented musician and close friend of mine, put together the King Of Belgium Band, named after my book, and John would be the headline star. Tickets sold in no time. In fact, we had to add a Sunday matinee show as well. We had fan-club presidents from all over Europe coming to the show and all of a sudden the media had discovered Elvis Presley's guitarist too.

To make a long story short, all of a sudden, John got invitations from literally everywhere: Germany, Switzerland, Austria, the UK, Holland, Japan even, Italy... and before I knew it, I was John's European manager. My wife Sonja, Geert and I set up a Web site for him and soon we booked John again ... and again and again. The fans couldn't seem to get enough of him. But how surprising can that be?

John Wilkinson is a fan. If you ever have the chance to visit his home, you'll see what I mean: beautiful plates of Elvis on the wall, hundreds of pictures in his music room, and stacks and stacks of scrapbooks. John knows what it is to be a fan of Elvis. He feels the love, and that message comes across to every audience he talks to.

In the meantime, my interest in the music of Elvis grew. I found myself collecting more than 3,000 records, all of his movie posters, thousands of pictures, hundreds of newspaper clippings ... and together with a group of seven top-notch friends, I decided to begin my own fanclub: "ElvisMatters," endorsed by John Wilkinson. This was three or four years ago. It's about Elvis matters and it's a statement too: Although it's been almost 30 years, Elvis still matters!

What does a fanclub do? Well, we publish magazines, we're active on the Internet, we travel to Memphis every year and we organize quality shows. One of the biggest shows we did back then was the very first reunion of the full TCB Band: James, Jerry, Glenn D., Ronnie and John Wilkinson. The moment John walked out on stage to reunite with his TCB buddies—for the first time since June 1977—is one of the highlights of my life. I thought the place came down. People were standing on their seats, clapping, crying, applauding for more, more, more. When John finished his third and last song, the showroom started echoing: "Johnny, Johnny, Johnny!" If ever there was a doubt in John's mind that the fans still care for him, there was the answer.

In 10 year's time, from my first contact with John to now, our friendship has grown. We understand each other without having to talk. I know how he feels about things and he knows what I feel for him, and his beautiful wife, Terry. In a way it's strange to say. After all, John was Elvis's guitarist for almost 10 years—but he truly is my best friend. My kids call him "uncle John" and I simply refer to him as "Johnny" or "Hey you." There's not a subject in the world we can't talk about. I can't begin to tell you how blessed I feel to have met John that evening in 1992. He has touched and changed my life forever. I am a better man for knowing John Wilkinson.

Being the president of Elvis Matters, I am in constant contact with all the other Elvis musicians. One of the shows we're currently working on features the Imperials, the Sweet Inspirations, Joe Guercio and a 75-piece orchestra, and the full TCB Band. Being able to do such top-class shows in sold-out venues in Holland and Belgium (and who knows where we'll end up), is a thrill I can't begin to explain. I cherish and love each and every musician who worked with Elvis. They are the only ambassadors of Elvis. They still are the backbone of his show.

James, man: You are truly a wizard on guitar. No one can top your style. Elvis wanted the best musicians in the world. It's no wonder that he handpicked you. You're a wonderful man and I love you. I miss you and Louise! Glenn D: Hey man, have I ever thanked you enough for making all these concerts we did such a success? You're top class, buddy. Thank you for everything you did for us. And Jerry: Thank you for those long conversations we've had and for opening up your heart to me. I love you, my friend! Ronnie, thank you for your kind friendship, for your hard work during our shows, for being who you are: my very special friend. You and Donna will always have a very special place in my heart. And Joe, Mr. Maestro, you made "it" happen, when we did the six concerts with the big orchestra. If it wasn't for you, we would've never been able to pull this off. You know how much we love you. You are the best!

And to John, a prince among men: Thank you for changing my life. I'll probably never be able to tell you how much you and Terry mean to me, my wife and our kids. We are so proud of you. Friends forever. No, make that: pals forever!

Peter Verbruggen
Mol, Belgium, January 21, 2006

John's Acknowledgements

FIRST, I WANT TO THANK my parents, Richard and Virginia Wilkinson for putting up with me during my battle to be a musician and for endorsing me. They encouraged me in ways that when they saw that music was going to be it, they said go ahead and be the best. And for the kind of upbringing they gave me and the kind of household I was in. Without mom and dad, who knows what I would've ended up doing.

I want to thank my loving, long-suffering wife Terry of 22 years for her support, not only through the rough times when I had my stroke but through all the times I was making music, for clapping and leading the audience on. She's a wonderful gal and I couldn't have made it without her.

Don and Myrna Roscoe, of Culver City, bless their hearts, they were there when I needed them most. Gordon Lightfoot, bless your heart old friend, the Kingston Trio, Bob Shane, Nick Reynolds, John Stewart, Dave Guard, the Limelighters, so many people. If I leave your name out, please don't feel like you've been slighted.

Adya Bryant, Mama, for all the times when I was first starting out with no money and no place to go and no place to eat. Your house was open and you fed us all.

Dave Peel, old friend, we made beautiful music together and hopefully we can again,

Also wanted to say thank you to all my schoolmates at Greenwood High School in Springfield, Mo., who followed my career and are my number-one fans. Anne Rittershouse, Jack and Carol

Acuff, Steve Moore, Bonnie and Bob Richardson, Don and Myrna Roscoe, Judy Nichols, Mike Lampy, all of you. Thank you for your support and all the loving letters and wonderful times you gave me when you'd come to see me perform no matter where I was.

Ray Walker, bass singer with the Jordanniares. Larry Geller, hair dresser and spiritual guide. Clair Brothers, our sound guys. Joe Guercio, who made things so easy for us. The unsung heroes of every show, the stagehands. If it wasn't for the stagehands, there wouldn't be no show. They're the ones who made sure there were lights backstage, that the curtain would rise, the lights were right. Special kudos to stagehands everywhere.

To Roy Orbison, Elvis's favorite singer and a good friend of mine. I miss him. I want everyone to know that Roy Orbison was Elvis's favorite singer.

Old friends of mine from the days in Culver City, playing the Tattle Tale and the VFW halls and all that kind of thing, who rushed to console me, and come over to the house and play piano and guitar and sing with me to get my spirits up. And would also come by to take me to my rehab sessions at the hospital when I was finally back home.

And Ron Goodman, my old buddy from when we were roommates in Ladara Heights, who played guitar and sang with me—a funny guy. He worked at Hughes the same time I did and was a John Stewart fan.

And to the Kingston Trio, my friends there and John Stewart.

And to all the fans around the world, in the States who have been so gracious as to invite me into their homes and their countries and cities for special things.

And to all the doctors—except for one, who was an IDIOT—special thanks.

And for everybody who buys this book, I hope you find it interesting. It's been a heck of ride for me. And I look forward to being in your town, and soon. If you want me, you know where to find me.

All the band, all the singers, and even the Colonel. All these wonderful people who have had (even a little bit) to do with my life, those little bits have turned into big bits.

And friends along the line, like meeting you, Nick. Now who knew that we'd meet and become good buddies, but I'm sure glad we did. And Peter Verbuggen, God love you man. Thank you for sharing your family and Sonja, your lovely wife, and three lovely kids, Jesse, Darja, Natya, and even your dog Ms. Nipper, my special little doggie. There's just too many people to thank.

A special thanks of course to the late Dr. F. Bion McCurrey, thank you. I know we'll meet again. I know where you are: You're playing piano for JD Sumner, I know you are. Just everyone who has had a piece of my life and has helped me become successful and has believed in me. All the way through and never gave up on me: thank you.

Last but not least—Elvis Presley, thank you very much. I know where you are, Boss, and I know one day I'll see you again. Thank you for giving my career a real meaning. I love you.

I'm just a lucky guy to have all of you as friends and we will meet again, I just know it. Thank you and hope you enjoy the book.

Nick's Acknowledgements

I'D LIKE TO THANK my parents, Brian and Linda Cendro, who always encouraged me to read, write, play and learn music, and paid for my journalism degree, which ensured that when an opportunity like this one came, I'd be ready to handle it.

Of course, big thanks to John Wilkinson for this incredible chance to tell his story. He's become like family to me, him and his wife, Terry. Thanks to them for their generosity and friendship (and patience!) while we worked on this book.

Thanks to James Hohner, my dear friend and brilliant musician, whose genius at art direction makes this book look so good!

Thanks to Sarah Humphries and John Wyatt for their invaluable help transcribing the interviews.

Thanks to Mike McConnell for being an Elvis fanatic.

Finally, thanks to the friend I never knew, Elvis Presley. Sitting and talking (and drinking!) with John, watching movies and concerts with him, and hearing his countless fascinating stories, I feel like I do know Elvis in some way. I agree with John that Elvis was touched and was truly a gift to the world, to enjoy and to emulate. To paraphrase a line from Lawrence Kasdan's screenplay, "The Big Chill": "There was something about him that was too good for this world."

Wherever you are, Mr. Presley, thank you for helping my writing career and I hope we've helped clear up some of the negative imagery conjured by tabloid-minded "historians" regarding the last decade of your career.

"There is nothing more notable in Socrates than that he found time, when he was an old man, to learn music and dancing, and thought it time well spent."

— Elvis Presley

Forward

Hello friends and fans,

The reason I wanted to tell this story is because there's been so much crap written about Elvis that I thought it was time that the real story of the real man be told from the perspective of a guy who longed to be a superstar also, and I wanted the fans to know that while you may look at him as a god, he's not. He's not a saint, he's not an angel. He's just as human as anyone else.

He cried, he laughed, he had his own personal demons like we all do. He was a real human being. He had his faults and he had his good points. But I thought it was important to get a book out. I know that the story we're telling in this book will be understood and read by many people, and they'll see—from the perspective of a guy who stood right behind him—the human side of Elvis.

He was human and he wasn't just a flash-in-the-pan hillbilly kid who got lucky: He was meant to be. He truly was a child of heaven. I wouldn't trade a minute of my time with him for $10 million. I think of him every day and I remember the effect he had on people.

When he sang, he was singing to every individual person in that auditorium. It could be 30,000 people or it could be 5,000 people. But every person felt like Elvis was singing right to him or her.

And I learned a lot by watching him. I learned for my own performances about how to work a stage, how to let people know I'm there for them.

"The only reason I'm on this stage up higher than you is so you can see me better. It doesn't mean I'm better than you. That's why we have a stage," he would say to the audience.

He loved his fans. He considered the fans to be an extended part of his family. There wasn't a thing in the world he wouldn't do for his fans. Even at the point in his life where his body was giving out and he didn't look real well, he still, every night, got up on stage and gave 150,000 percent, even to the point he was in such pain you could see it in his face. But he still kept singing for them.

He had an appreciation for all types of music. If he were alive today, he'd still be performing probably, but he wouldn't be doing "Heartbreak Hotel" and "Hound Dog" as a staple. He'd be doing gospel music and country music. But he'd listen to, I'm sure, everybody who was out there performing now to see what they're doing. And see what America and the rest of the world is listening to. And I'm sure he'd try to look at that and say, "Is this concept in a song something I can incorporate into what I can do?"

He loved music. He had a record collection that included everything from the old gospel groups to Tom Jones and the Kingston Trio. He had my records and he had a lot of symphonic music. He really was a very complex man. Here is my story and his.

— John Wilkinson
   March 5, 2005

"Ambition is a dream with a V8 engine."
— ELVIS PRESLEY

The Shrine Mosque, Springfield, MO.

Prologue

— 1 —

MAY 17, 1956, SPRINGFIELD, MO.
Through the warm shine of the afternoon's dusking sun, the boy and his bike rode over dirt, grass and cement, skirted obstacles, past familiar sights, toward destiny. The inevitable warmth of summer nights to come flirted with the boy's senses this fine spring day.

Excitement, guilt, determination ... the 10-year-old pounding heart couldn't quite sort all these feelings *and* furiously pedal the bicycle could it?

The boy absent-mindedly recounted what spurred his quest, excited by the mission; guilty for not telling his parents where he was going; and determined to accomplish the task he'd set. It started after school one day, while having a snack, catching some local news.

* * * * * *

An Elvis Presley concert tonight, right here in Springfield at the old Shrine Mosque where the boy and his father had recently performed for a talent show. The kids at school were talking about it. The papers and radio advertised it. The parents didn't quite approve of it. The boy, however, didn't know what to make of the kid from Tupelo and his music.

But one thing did bother the boy, very much: that TV footage of him banging on that beautiful Martin D-18 acoustic guitar ...

banging on it. Beating on it! An instrument you stroke lovingly ... and what is rock and roll? This guy's abusing a beautiful instrument ... and the boy worked his tail off on the banjo and guitar ... and he's on TV ...

It just didn't sit right with the boy. Beating on a Martin D-18 like that. And that rock and roll ... well, the music wasn't really bad. It was actually pretty ... "wild." But you just don't beat an instrument that we'd all like to have like that. It's like beating a dog.

He pedaled on, knowing he'd have to be back before mom and dad knew where he'd gone. He also wondered ... what if he actually did get to speak to Mr. Presley? He looked a bit rough ... the sideburns ... the long hair ... the leather jacket. Like Brando in "The Wild One." Will he be cruel?

"What are you rebelling against?"

"What have you got?"

With a complete naturalness that would serve him all his life, John Wilkinson focused away from distractions and back to his goal: to find Mr. Presley and to tell him that he couldn't play guitar worth a damn.

— 2 —

As John rounded St. Louis Street, the old Shrine Mosque waited for him. The large brick building with its exotic domes inspired images of Ali Baba and magic carpets. He'd always loved the building, staring at it from the car when he was very young, wondering what it was.

Recently, he got his chance to see the place from the inside, performing with his father. How he'd wanted to search the place then! Were there secret rooms?

As John entered, he could hear the music from the performance stage. It was Hank Snow! Hank Snow was rehearsing! Nervous once again, John quickly remembered his mission and that the dressing rooms were on the second floor. It was probably the best place to look first.

The music from below calmed John a bit as he cautiously looked into one room after another. Perhaps Mr. Presley wasn't even in the building. Perhaps he was still at his hotel or having a dinner before his performance.

John surprised himself by feeling disappointment rather than relief that he wasn't there. He really did want to meet Mr. Presley! He didn't want to be off the hook! Better go ... but first, one more door to check on the left ...

John peered into the doorway and froze. There he is. He's a kid! Wearing jeans and denim jacket ... red-checked shirt, saddle-shoed feet on the dressing room table, hamburgers scattered about, leaning back in a folding chair, sipping cola ...

"You're Elvis Presley."

"I know that."

Smart ass," John thought.

"I'm John Wilkinson. I'd like to talk to you for a minute if I could. You got a minute?"

Elvis smiled, sideburns, neatly combed, beautiful.

"Sure. Come on in."

Elvis stood and shook John's hand as he nervously entered. An old Gibson J-45, another beautiful acoustic, leaned in the corner.

Bet he beats on that, too.

"Sit down."

John sat, unable to stop looking at Elvis.

"Mr. Presley ..."

"Johnny, that's my daddy. I'm Elvis."

John was raised never to call a grownup by his or her first name without permission. Elvis certainly recognized that and smiled again. John realized he now had to work to maintain his ire toward this young man and his treatment of that Martin, but he found it suddenly difficult. He wasn't some rude thug. He did speak coherently, despite some of the gibberish of his vocal performances. In fact ... Elvis Presley seemed like he might be a really nice person.

"Where do you go to school? How old are you? Do you live in town? What do your parents do?"

John answered these questions masking some surprise, not only because they were being asked at all but also because Elvis was genuinely interested. John could always smell a condescension or patronizing stance, even at ten. He was a precocious only child with extremely educated parents and it activated an instinctive judge of character—including the ability to recognize insincerity.

Not here. As John talked about his school, his home and his parents, Elvis listened, his eyes focused on him.

John saw sincerity in those eyes. Elvis told a little about where he came from. Of course, that had already been printed. Son of a sharecropper, dirt poor. John stole another glance at the old J-45 leaning against the wall, suddenly almost ashamed of his assumptions about this polite, friendly gentleman. But he'd come here for a reason and it was time for that reason to be made known.

"Elvis, the real reason I came down to see you was because I've got to tell you something."

"What?"

"You can't play guitar worth a damn."

Elvis looked at the boy strangely, both insulted and amused.

"You think you can play better than me?"

"I know I can."

"How old are you?"

"Ten."

"And you can play guitar better than me, huh?"

"Absolutely. Mind if I borrow your guitar over there for a minute?"

Elvis smiled and nodded.

John strode to the old J-45, strapped it on and put on the set of fingerpicks he always carried. And he played. And he sang. And Elvis watched and listened.

"You're pretty good."

"I know," John answered with a mischievous smile in retaliation to the earlier "I know" from Elvis.

Elvis was impressed as John continued, his right-hand fingers dancing around the soundhole, fingerstyle, five years of banjo and guitar work now on display for Elvis Presley.

"You know what you're doing on that guitar, don't you?"

"Yeah, I think so. I love to play guitar and I love to sing songs

"... and I like your songs."

Elvis's soon-to-be-immortal grin betrayed true appreciation. This boy could play!

"Who are you?"

A couple of very big guys were suddenly in the room and halted the moment.

"What are you doing here?"

"Now, just a minute here," Elvis said, standing. "This here's a friend of mine. His name is John Wilkinson and he just gave me a guitar lesson."

The two large men, obviously their job to see to Elvis's well being, looked young John up and down but ceded to the man who would be king.

"Well, OK, fine, but Elvis, you know you've got a sound check. Kid, you're gonna have to get out of here."

Wonderful moments ... why are they always so short? John set the guitar down and stood.

"OK, take it easy, I'm leavin'," he said with a boy's disappointment.

John started to move toward the door.

"Johnny, come here," Elvis said.

The young boy approached the young man who gave him a friendly hug.

"You know what, John? I just know deep in my heart we're going to meet again."

"Well, Elvis, I hope so," John answered, brightening. "I hope you have a good show tonight."

"Are you coming to the show?"

"No, I don't have tickets and my folks would probably not even like that I'm here."

John thought of his parents, bless them, very conservative people. Elvis Presley, in their minds, was not exactly a good role model for their young, impressionable son. But too late ... Elvis rubbed off on John right away and he stuck. They shook hands, John again seeing the sincere eyes of Elvis Presley.

"I do hope we meet again, Elvis," John thought. "And I look forward to that day."

— 3 —

With renewed joy, inspired fulfillment of a mission accomplished accompanied by unexpected pleasures, John pedaled the direction from whence he came. He had accomplished his mission. He got to tell Elvis he couldn't play guitar and showed him how it was done.

He pondered the man he'd just met. John expected to find a real black-leather hoodlum type and realized the graciousness of the man took him completely off guard. John felt momentary shame, unable to answer why he'd expected him to be anything other than a nice guy.

He seems lonely. Like he really welcomed me because I was somebody other than the people in his circle ... an outsider, who wasn't after anything.

* * * * *

Today, John reflects on that magic day, remembering thinking to himself as he pedaled, "That kid don't have anybody to play with.

"I didn't ask him for an autograph, for instance. And he reminded me of that later on in our relationship. I finally got one from him. It's up there on the wall. It's a genuine autograph.

"But I remember thinking, that kid don't have anybody to play with. And the way I read his upbringing, he didn't have—they weren't full of kids like you and I had when we were growing up. You know, there was always enough guys or girls around to get up a baseball game or go out and fly kites in the park or play tag or something. He didn't have that. I did. You did, where you were brought up, and me. He didn't have that, and I got thinking, this kid don't have anybody to play with. And he needed somebody from outside to talk to that didn't want anything from him.

"I didn't come in and say, 'Elvis, you know what? I desperately need a new bicycle because I've got a scratch on mine.' I didn't want nothing from him. I wanted to tell him something, not ask him for anything. I know that stuck with him all during the years that we knew each other, because I was one of the few in the inner circle and the people who worked around him who never asked for anything.

"I never asked for a raise, either. I got them. But I never asked for anything. I told him when I finally got with him in the concert years:

"*I'm here for one reason: to play music for you. I'll be here for you through thick and thin. Whatever you need, if nobody else can do it for you, you come to me and I will make sure what you need happens.*

"That was the kind of relationship we had. He knew he could count on me. I was proud to be that kind of a person for him."

Mom and Dad on meeting Elvis

As unbelievable as it seems, it wasn't until very recently that John told his parents the story of how he first met Elvis.

"I was telling my parents about the new book, and the story is in there about how I went and met him down there.

"And I told my mother, 'There's a story in there I bet you don't know anything about.' And she said, 'Oh, yeah? What's that?' And I told her about how I first met Elvis. She said, 'Did you really?' I said, 'I did.' She said, 'You never said a word to us.' I said, 'I know. I know I didn't. Because I didn't think you'd appreciate it.'

"You know, me taking off like that and going on my own all the way downtown on my bike, and especially to go talk to this greasy, long-haired guy, you know, what they figured he was.

"I don't know. To me, it was personal, I guess. It was between me and him. It would be like a confidence that you would tell one of your best friends, that nobody else would need to know about but that you'd have to tell somebody to get it out of you. And I sort of looked at my meeting with him that way. It was personal.

"And because he wasn't accepted, because not very many of my friends—well, a few did—but not very many of my friends would have thought Elvis was anything. So it wouldn't have meant anything to them. They probably would have laughed at me."

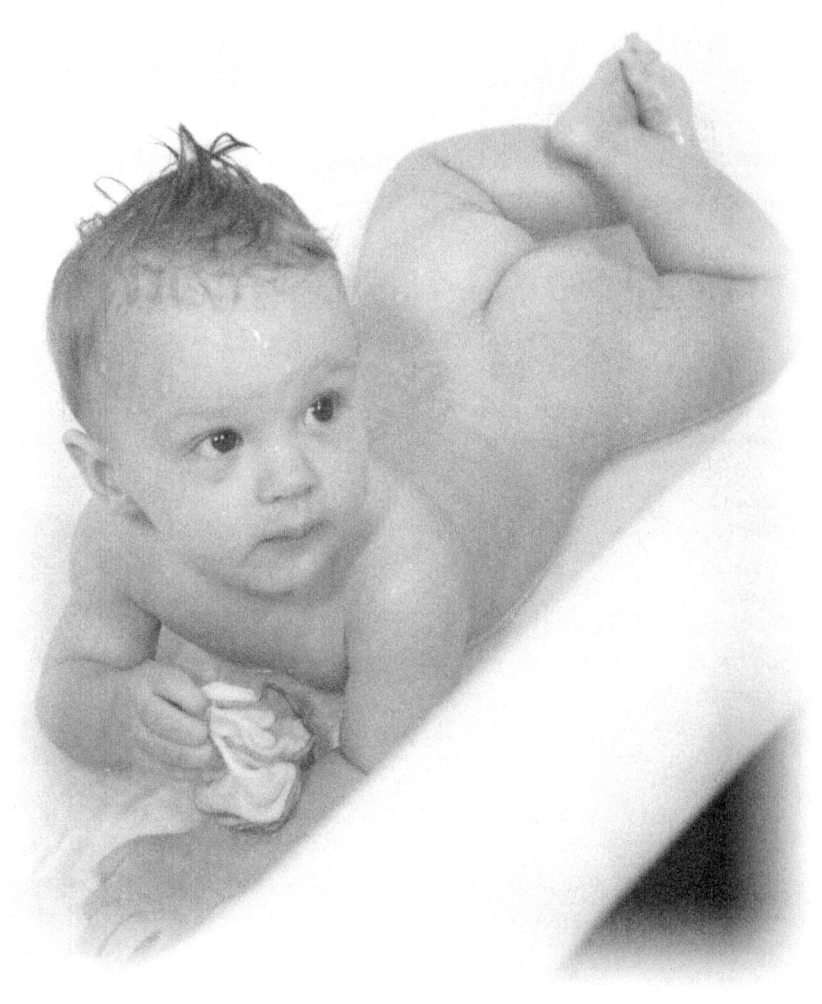

Baby John Wilkinson.

CHAPTER 1

Earliest Memories

— 1 —

Born on the 3rd of July, 1945, John Wilkinson still has memories of being in his crib, which, to his already-flexing mind, could actually be a jail, a fort ... anything he wanted.

"I remember the slats, the rails in between ... I remember when I got too big for that," he recalls, "and my mom and dad going out and getting me a single bed—that was big time for me!"

John recently moved back to his childhood home in Springfield. The big mid-western house with its two stories and basement was built in 1910 between to other houses from the same builder, each occupied by old ladies when John was a boy.

Richard Wilkinson, John's father, was a professor of psychology at Southwest Missouri State College (now a university), and he actually started the psychology department at the university around 1939. The department exists today because of Richard.

"I'm very proud of my father, very proud," John says. "My mom was a full-time housewife, a homemaker, and anybody who tells you that being a housewife isn't real work is crazy. It's a full-time job and if you get someone like me, it's even more a full-time job! She was always a wonderful cook and we always had lots of good food, plenty of it, more if you wanted."

John's mother, Virginia, was also a college graduate, with a degree in geology from Drury College, of Springfield.

Richard was born in Youngstown, Ohio, and raised in Warren,

Ohio. Virginia was born in Edna, Texas, and her family relocated to Springfield. Virginia's father was a doctor and had his own practice in Springfield for many years before retiring.

Richard moved to Springfield after serving in the U.S. Navy, when he was offered a job as an instructor at the Southwest State College. Recently, Dr. Wilkinson's name was added to the University's wall of fame.

Obviously, with such academic parents, it is not surprising that even at the age of nine, young John Wilkinson had an upbringing that would result in assertiveness and confidence.

Growing up in the 1940s and early 1950s, John enjoyed a childhood similar to most of his generation.

"I loved to play cowboys and Indians, cops and robbers," he remembers. "My favorite shows were Roy Rogers, Gene Autry, Wild Bill Hickock and the Cisco Kid, all 30-minute shows on TV."

Before TV, many of these shows were broadcast on radio. John recalls enjoying such mystery shows as "I Love a Mystery," "Young Dr. Malone," "The Shadow," as well as comedies such as, "Jack Benny."

"I'd listen to the shows with my parents and alone. I still have some old recordings of 'The Lone Ranger.'"

John recalled owning a little red cowboy hat with a strap under the chin and a six-shooter at his side.

"I could be anybody," he says. "Wild Bill, the Cisco Kid, Matt Dillon ... I still remember the first "Gunsmokes" on the radio and it wasn't James Arness. And (I remember) William Conrad, he was the voice of the Lone Ranger on the radio."

John and his friends acted out the radio show they heard the night before, each taking parts and reenacting the drama. The world was a beautiful place.

"And climbing trees. I remember we had a couple of trees in the front yard that I could climb and get up into the branches there, and that was fun. I also remember in the backyard, there was two cherry trees, and when the cherries would come in season I would get Daddy's 6-foot ladder, and I would go up and pick cherries and put them in a box and take them inside.

"We had a housekeeper, Miss Carden, I remember—a real sweet lady—and every Wednesday she came to help Mom with the housework and she'd make cherry pies with the cherries I'd picked out of our own trees. And there's nothing I like better than cherry pie—cherry pie *á la mode*—let's be honest here, a little scoop of ice cream—a big scoop of ice cream on the side.

"And she would make a pastry shell with cinnamon sugar for me when I came home from school. And Miss Carden was always there on Wednesdays when I came home from school. I got out at 3:15. And we didn't live that far from—my high school was on the campus of Southwest Missouri State University, and I would walk to school. My dad and I would walk to school together. We would walk home together sometimes, or if dad had to stay later, I would just walk home on my own.

"In those days, we didn't have to worry about kidnapping off the streets and these animals that are picking up these kids and doing God-knows-what to them and then killing them and all that. What ever happened to those days, man? I miss those days. I mean, we in my generation here, we look and say, 'Those were the good old days. Those were simpler times.'

"We see it that way. But those times were not always that simple for moms and dads of kids my age. But to us, looking back now when we're living now, the late '50 and early '60s, the mid-'50s on were the good old days. It was a time of innocence."

— 2 —

John recalls, to the best of his objective ability, that he was a happy child, very content, very warm and safe with his parents at his house. His parents were very loving people and John recalls great times and wonderful friends. And he was an only child, which often results in unique personality types, not unlike a certain singer John would soon meet. Like many only children, John was as self-reliant as he was social.

"I became an avid reader when I was very young," he recalls. "I liked to read anything I could get my hands on and that's true to this day. I love to read. I'll read anything from a cookbook to a telephone directory!"

Included in his reading material were comic books, although John's parents didn't approve of war comic books. They did give him subscriptions to Little Lulu and Bugs Bunny. He would also borrow super hero comics from his friend, enjoying the late golden age adventures of Superman and Batman.

"Sometimes I would come home at lunch at the lunch break from grade school and my mom had a little sandwich maker, and I would make grilled-cheese sandwiches," John remembers. "Grilled cheese and peanut butter and jelly. Yeah, and cottage cheese with a big old glob of applesauce right in the middle of it. I loved to cook, even to this day. But I liked to come home in those days, because I really enjoyed being in that house. It wasn't just a house; it was a home. My mom and dad made it a home, and we were very happy there. They would read to me or they would play games with me—board games like checkers, or Parchisi, or any of those, Scrabble—we were a family."

The Wilkinsons also owned a cabin on the Finley River, a place called Lindenlure, and they'd go there on weekends sometimes to vacation or canoe.

"I loved to canoe. We'd go up the river. We'd take picnic lunches up on the sandbars and do that. Sometimes, I'd take a rod and reel and do a little fishing, catch perch, bass—small ones, you know. It was a little bitty river. I think it winds up into the White River or the James River, and eventually winds up in the Mississippi River. I loved Lindenlure. It was fun to go down there, and go hiking and that kind of thing. Go up and play badminton—we had a badminton set we put up in the grassy area above our cabin—and we played badminton, Mom and Dad and me.

"We did a lot of things as a family. I remember the wintertime, when we would get snow, enough snow to where I'd use my dad's old American Flyer sled. They would pull me on the sled up and down the street. The kids and I, the neighborhood kids, we'd build snow forts and have snowball fights and build snowmen. I said, it was an age of innocence, because kids don't do that anymore, I don't think. It was a fun time. My childhood was—I couldn't have asked for a better childhood. I had everything I needed. They made sure I had everything I needed. I wanted a horse at one point; I never got a horse. I was very mistreated!

"But I had everything I ever needed and at Christmas time, I usually got pretty much my whole wish list, and remember believing in Santa—and now of course I still believe in the spirit of Santa. I remember being very upset when somebody at school said, 'There is no such thing as Santa Claus.' And I remember throwing a punch at that guy, too. 'What are you talking about? Hell, yes, there's a Santa Claus. I can show you the reindeer hoof prints on my roof in the snow!' I was adamant about that!

"On rainy days, I would read all day long. I remember in the dining room of the house in Springfield there, the sun would come in through the south window in the dining room. And where the dining room table was, there'd be huge shots of lights there from the sun, and I'd sit in that sun, nice and warm on a winter day, and I'd read. And Mom would make up some popcorn and we'd have popcorn and 7-Ups and I'd sit there and read all day long. I loved the Sherlock Holmes books. I'd get those at the little Elm Street branch library. I'd bring a bunch of books home and take them back in a few days. I learned to read at a very early age. And I'm very thankful for that. I learned to entertain myself.

"My childhood—I couldn't have asked for a better childhood. No kid could have. I was very lucky. My whole life, I've been very, very fortunate, very lucky."

— 3 —

Even with great friends, loving parents and a very active life, it still didn't take long for a very young John Wilkinson to find music. It wasn't too hard for music to find John because there was always music in his home.

John's parents loved the classics, like Brahms, Beethoven, Bach and Mozart. He recalls Springfield having a wonderful public broadcasting station and listeners could get all of that music on the radio.

"There was always music in the house," John says. "My mom and dad liked to listen to opera. I'm not a big fan of opera then, nor am I now. But I recognize it as a beautiful art form.

"We had a piano in the house, and I'd noodle on that a little bit. I was never a piano player. Not really. I did take some piano lessons from a dear departed friend now, Mr. Will Adler, and I remember Miss Wise was a music teacher, and I took piano lessons from her."

When John was about five, he was introduced to music at Greenwood Elementary, where his teacher was Mr. McCurrey.

"All the classes, kindergarten through 12th grade, you always had a music course, and it wasn't anything you got graded on. You'd sing. Mr. McCurrey would hand out songbooks, and he would play the songs and we'd sing."

John found that he loved singing. Mr. McCurrey taught his students to sing harmony and soon *Dr.* McCurrey (who soon got his doctorate shortly after John made his acquaintance), would single John out to sing solos, noticing him as early as kindergarten.

"I didn't have much of a voice when I was in kindergarten, I'm sure. But he could see that I loved music. And after school was out, sometimes when I'd be walking past that room on my way out of the building, he'd call to me,

"Hey, Johnny, come here. I want you to listen to this. Can you sing these words?"

"And this was about 6th grade on. Wonderful guy, Mac was. This was really under way when I was about 12 or 13. He'd ask if I could sing to his piano part.

"Yeah, I can do that."

"I'd never really learned how to read music. I can a little bit now, but I learned everything by ear. And he showed me how to play the melody on the piano, so it stuck."

Johnny not only loved music but also soon realized he had a natural inclination for it.

"I was a one-take guy all the time," John remembers. "He'd play the melody ...

"OK, I can follow that."

"You have a wonderful voice, John. I hope you use it.'"

Indeed, it was Dr. McCurrey who got John actively involved in doing music. At home, it was listening.

"I'd listen to—I had my grandmother's old AM radio, and I'd turn it on real soft and I could pick up WSM in Nashville at night sometimes. I'd listen; I'd hear a song there, some of the old country things, and in the morning I'd remember it and I'd go down to the piano and try to pick up the melody on there, and then a little later on I transferred that to the guitar."

His parents did not force John's early piano lessons on him. They recognized their son's affinity for music and provided him with the tools to learn music if he wanted to. John realizes that they knew that if they'd forced him, it wouldn't be fun.

"I looked at music then as I do now: Whenever it becomes a job, I'll quit. But the piano lessons really gave me an insight into what I was hearing on the radio, the chords, the melody structures, putting them both together, left hand and right hand.

"So, being actively involved that way, with the little exercises Miss Wise would give me, and then later on Mac and Mr. Adler would show me, I got more involved with piano, not to make piano my prime instrument because it never was. But without that, I never would have been able to do as well on guitar as I have."

Love of music and love of playing music is good enough for one's self. However, the pleasant feeling young John enjoyed from the attention was not lost on him.

"We'd be in the music room and all the class would be in their chairs on the different levels there, and Mac would say:

"*John, come down here. I want you to sing this and they're going to hum the background for you.*"

"And I'd sing and I'm thinking—I noticed the girls looking—and I'm thinking, wait a minute here. I got something here! Even at that young age, I'm thinking, 'Hey, this is alright.'

"There I was, Johnny Wilkinson, I'm singing and he likes me.

My instructor likes me. He likes what I'm doing. I'm big time. Yeah, I remember that. I got a buzz off that."

John's early success in music depended on both his own interest and aptitude, and the encouragement and attention of his parents and teachers. The adults in John's early life factored strongly in his progress.

"The way I was brought up, with two wonderful parents, and my instructors at Greenwood, was all very positive influences on me," John says. "They made learning fun. Whether it was music or anything else, they made it fun."

But where would the fun of music lead? It was still a time before pop music caused young men to learn guitar and form rock groups. In John's world, he looked up to a local old-time country singer who lived in Springfield, Red Foley, and the folk group, The Weavers. In the early 1950s, the Weavers were a group John listened to for pleasure and the fact that their songs were relatively easy to learn didn't hurt, either.

"The songs were easy," he recalls. "Anybody can sing them. I liked the harmonies and I could hear the guitars, the acoustic guitars. It was that kind of music, because of where I was raised, Springfield was the center of country music. All the country stars came through Springfield. They would all perform in Springfield. This was long before Branson became a hot box of country music—the new Nashville, if you will.

"I would hear them and I would see them. They would perform on the local news to promote the shows they were doing. So, literally I was surrounded with music. I was surrounded with it and there was no hope. Just like the boys at the Alamo, there was no hope. Music was around me all the time and it was my downfall in school because music got in the way. I didn't care about anything else except music."

The idea that music would be John's life hit him at the ripe old age of five. It was while still in grade school that John found his instrument. In country and folk music, unlike the rock music of later, the main instrument is not necessarily the guitar. There is the banjo, the bass, the mandolin and the fiddle. John already played piano and sang. But that first old guitar did not let him get away.

"I was in grade school and I remember Mac had an old guitar and there was an old banjo in his office, where the band instruments were kept," John recalls. "I remember that was the first guitar I ever played. It was an old Silvertone perhaps, I'm not sure. And I remember taking that guitar out to where the piano was in that classroom and I hit the note on the guitar, low E the first string, and tapped it on the piano. OK, that's an E; I know what that is. Then dum, dee. That's A. I know what that is on the piano. So, I learned right off how to tune the thing.

"And I started listening to music on the radio and in the classroom, and I would make the chords myself on the piano because Mac had taught me how to do that. And I would take those pieces of knowledge and actually take it to the guitar."

Despite his experience with other instruments, there was indeed something about that guitar.

Among God's creatures, two— the dog and the guitar—have taken all the sizes and all the shapes, in order not to be separated from the man.

"I felt like it was a real personal instrument. I couldn't carry a piano around with me. But a guitar, you could stick that in your bicycle basket. I felt like it was a buddy, that guitar. That old beat-up guitar of Mac's, and it just felt like my best friend. Like my best buddies in school, who are still best buddies to me, some of them. But that guitar felt like a real personal thing to me. And every day I'd go in and play on that guitar."

John wasn't sure where the guitar came from. He suspects it was Mac's, kept in his office at the school perhaps because there wasn't room at his home. It hardly mattered. Mac didn't mind John's interest one bit.

"No, in fact, he'd encourage me!
"Johnny, I think you've got a friend there."
"Well, I think so, Dr. McCurrey."

"Later on, as we were in high school, we could call him Mac. We got to be very good friends. Wonderful, wonderful man. I can still see his picture in my mind right now.

"Had it not been for Mac and Miss Wise, and later on Will Adler and various other teachers and influences, I would not probably have enjoyed music as much and decided music had to be a real part of me.

"Music was going to be my way of expressing myself. And I felt like I had to do that. And it was another mission, if you will, because I never knew my birth parents. I was adopted when I was two months old. Maybe they had—I know they were in the Navy. They were killed in a car crash in Washington, D.C., and left me as an orphan. And then fortunately, Richard and Virginia Wilkinson came and adopted me. I was a lucky kid.

"Anyway, whether my birth parents were musically inclined or not, I don't know. I have no idea, but it came so easily to me. Music always, from the very earliest times when I was five years old, it just came naturally. It wasn't a job. It wasn't hard for me. Music, I could hear. My ear—still to this day, I have a real good ear. Everything I learned I learned by ear. I would put those things together in my head and translate that to the guitar—transpose that into the guitar, is the word. But that had to be my earliest recollections."

*"I've always been a dreamer.
When I was young, I used to read comic books
and go to the movies, and I was the hero."*

— ELVIS PRESLEY

John's childhood was filled with music.

CHAPTER 2

Growing up music

— 1 —

JOHN PROGRESSION FROM the personal discovery of playing music was soon accompanied by a personal pleasure in hearing—and learning—from other musicians. He watched the Grand Ole Opry, fascinated by the banjo one night. Conveniently, Mac also stored an old banjo back in his office.
"*Mind if I try that?*"
"*Sure, Johnny, anything you want.*"
"First, he tuned it for me," John remembers. "And I took it to the piano and once again, I hit the note on the banjo to make it sound on the piano. I learned how to tune the banjo. And then by listening to Lester Flatt and Earl Scruggs.
"*Man, he's doing something there.*"
John recalled his pleasure in Flatt and Scruggs as early as six. He'd watch them on TV and they often performed in Springfield. But it was the glow of a 13-inch black-and-white General Electric television set where Johnny's eyes and ears absorbed the fingers and noises of Mr. Flatt and Mr. Scruggs.
"I watched Mr. Scruggs with the banjo and I saw he was using three fingers. He was doing something there. And come to find out later through Mac, it's called Bluegrass.
"*It's called what?*"
"*It's called Bluegrass. That's the style that Mr. Scruggs is playing.*"
"*Well, I'll be darned.*"

"So I began watching and listening again, and my ear was highly developed for some reason. And I'd listen to him play and I would try to duplicate that, and I was able to do it on one chord: the open G chord. So I got that. And I started playing around on the neck finding other chords. And I think Mac had an old Mel Bay How-to-Play-the-Banjo book or something and I looked in there and, 'Alright, I know that's a G chord and that's a C chord.' So I could get it I'd go to the little piano out there, da da da da da. So that's a C chord. How do I make that on the banjo? That's how I learned the chords on the banjo was by listening and taking notes I could make on the piano and putting them to the banjo. So I learned all my chords. And I knew how to play scales on the piano, so I learned how to play scales on the banjo the same way. Basically, that's what Bluegrass picking's all about: scales, arpeggios and the chord patterns. So by the time I was seven or eight I really got pretty good on both instruments, and Mac noticed.

"*Wow, I didn't have anything to do with you learning how to play those things. How'd you do it?*"

"*I made use of your music room. You told me I could come in here and play anytime I wanted.*"

And that is how the man who would play with Elvis learned those instruments. Thankfully, for the background of Miss Wise on the piano, Mac with his generous encouragement of voice, guitar and banjo, and later on, Mr. Adler, who was an old family friend, "now deceased, bless his heart.

"But with that kind of background and listening to the music, it just came so naturally to me. It really did. It wasn't something that I had to do. It was completely extracurricular. I wasn't getting graded on it in school.

"*That looks like fun. I think I can do that, let me try.*"

— 2 —

John found that he was an only child regarding his interest in music, as well. None of the other kids in the neighborhood were musically inclined. Their interests lay in sports, football, baseball, basketball. John simply had no interest in any sport save tennis, as he got older.

Meanwhile, John's development on banjo and guitar progressed simultaneously although he felt he had the guitar down by the time he noticed the banjo—as many six-year olds might! And what was the first song John recalls learning on guitar?

"Strangely enough, it was a song called 'Aura Lee,' and we know that today as 'Love Me Tender.' I learned that song because I would hear my mom singing it in the kitchen. She wasn't a great singer or anything, but she'd sing while she was washing the dishes or preparing dinner.

"And she'd sing this old song and I really liked it. And I remember going to the piano in our living room at the house in Springfield and thinking that sounds real pretty. And I'd put the chords to it the way I would hear the song and it turned out that they were right, you know. The majors and the minors and all that.

"*Mom, where'd you get that song? I like that song.*"

"*Well, that's an old, old song, Johnny. I was singing that when I was in school about your age.*"

"And she wrote down the words for me. And I'd sing that song, and I sang it for Mac, as a matter of fact, when I played it on guitar. I played the chords on guitar backing me up. And Mac was very impressed."

And Johnny knew a good thing when he had it. He never felt insecure or self-conscious while singing and playing, unlike so many highly successful artists.

"I felt real confident because I felt like I—of course, you never know everything you need to know about any instrument, no matter how you old get. If you ask Mr. Scruggs, he'll still tell you he don't know everything about a banjo. I don't believe that, but he'll tell you that.

"Anyway, I felt confident. Also, nobody else played in school—I was it. I had a corner on the market, if you will. And I loved to perform, even from those early days, when Mac would single me out to come down and sing solos. I felt very confident. I never felt self conscious about it that people would laugh at me or anything. People would hear me and they'd say, 'There's some talent there.'

"Mrs. Wilkinson, I'm keeping Johnny after school," Mac said into the phone. "He hasn't done anything wrong. He's just over here playing on this guitar and he's having fun. And I'll make sure he gets home OK."

It was either the eighth or the ninth Christmas that offered the new Silvertone guitar sitting against the tree. Right out of the Sears catalog.

"I would like to have a guitar of my own. I'm really enjoying playing Mr. McCurrey's old guitar over there. I'd like to have one of my own here."

"We'll see if Santa can come up with one."

"My own guitar! Santa Claus, alright! There IS a Santa Claus! I knew my folks had gotten it for me. But that was a very exciting time for me. I had my own guitar. And you couldn't keep that guitar away from me for nothing. Homework? What homework? I got a guitar to play. That guitar, all my life, has gotten in the way of a lot of things, you know?

"But I don't have any regrets at all. Thanks to that old beat-up guitar of Mac's there in the music room in Springfield in Greenwood High School. And my folks noticed—I didn't have a banjo of my own until I was, I don't know, 13 or so, I suppose. Maybe that's when I got my first Kay banjo, and again, right out of the Sears catalog. But Mac let me take that banjo home a couple times, his. I would play, and my folks were kind of amazed."

"Where'd you learn to do that, Johnny?"

"I listen, I watch. Everything I ever learned to do, Mom and Dad, in music, I learned by watching and listening, watching others, and trying to do what they did."

Seeing music performed on television, seeing people actually play, acted like a visual aid for John's learning. If John had any questions about a chord or something, he'd watch the guitar players—especially Dave Guard, of the Kingston Trio.

"I'd watch his hands. Uh ha. Uh ha. That's where he's going on that. And I'd hit it on my guitar. That's got to be it. I'd see things that I might have missed by just hearing it on the radio, by watching. I knew there were chords someplace that I didn't know about.

I watched him play. I'd keep my eyes on him."

— 3 —

John's main musical influences in those formative years included bluegrass, country and gospel music. John later learned he and Elvis shared yet another commonality in their childhoods: enjoying black church music.

"Some of those old preachers down there could play guitar. I mean, they could play guitar. And I got heavy influence from the rhythm patterns. Much like Elvis did. But I would watch them and I would listen to them and I would copy as close as I could. But again, I would go and watch what they were doing. Sneak into some of their church services on occasion—when I was supposed to be in Sunday school, for instance at First Calvary Presbyterian Church. A lot of times I didn't show up.

"I'd sneak over there and I'd go inside, and of course I was the only white face there, but I was a little boy. And I'd watch, and I'd watch, and I'd see the old preacher. He had—I didn't even know what an electric guitar was but I noticed something dragging off the back of his guitar and it was plugged into something. And I thought, 'What's that about?' Some kind of a thing then went across the soundhole the first pick-ups ever, I guess.

"I'd watch. And I'd watch his hands as he'd slap the rhythms and then strum. And I'd take that knowledge with me back home. The rhythms. The other styles that I was doing—the heavy influence was fingerpicking. And that's what I was concentrating on, not so much as the rhythm, but when I heard the old preachers playing, I'd watch them and I would pick it up. So I started learning rhythm patterns rather than just doing the fingerpicking things that I was doing."

Unlike so many guitar players, it seems John never was a strummer. His right hand—the thumb, the index and middle fingers—was much more demanding.

"That's the way I started out. And that's one of the things that attracted Elvis to me, the fact that I could finger pick. And also that on some of my records, there's some heavy rhythm playing. I learned that by watching and listening.

"And I remember later on when I met my heroes the Kingston Trio, I remember telling them, 'You know, fellows, what you've done for me, or to me, you know, I've got all your albums, I've learned all your songs'—and that was to prove to be very useful a little later on. I forget the song that was so difficult for me at the time because I was hearing the melody and I knew the basic chords but there were some little passing chord things in there and I told Mr. Guard, I call him Dave, 'Finally when I saw you on TV, the Ed Sullivan Show or the Dorsey Brothers or whatever it was, I finally saw what you were doing on guitar and I was able to transpose that to my own guitar. Now I know what you're doing. You can't fool me no more, Dave!'

"So, actually television in those days for me, it was a visual aid for me, to watch my favorites do the things that I was trying to do myself. It made me even more determined to become more proficient on guitar and banjo."

While all this music enriched John's life, one must remember that rock and roll did not yet permeate everything. John's love of music originally had nothing to do with rock and roll, something unfathomable today. It seems everyone who learns guitar today, learns because of rock and roll or some derivative of it. John learned because he loved music and he loved to make music. Almost no guitar players who learn because of rock and roll play fingerstyle. Yet John never seemed to consider not playing fingerstyle because of the country, western and folk music that surrounded him instead of rock and roll.

Nonetheless, rock and roll did catch up with John and the world soon enough in the form of a young, beautiful, soulful talent from Memphis. That's all right, mama.

*"I never did sing that much in my life.
The only time I ever sung maybe was in a little variety show
at school ... maybe once every couple of years.
"I had an old $20 guitar, sounded like somebody beatin'
on a bucket maybe, or somethin'."*

— Elvis Presley

Young John Wilkinson, musician.

CHAPTER 3

The horizon of music expands

— 1 —

THE RADIO MADE JOHN AWARE of Elvis Presley for the first time. It was a live broadcast of the Louisiana Hayride. The Hayride was a less glamorous version of the Grand Ole Opry, broadcast from Shreveport, LA. Sometimes, the Hayride broadcast its live shows from WSM, their remote facility, and John could pick it up on his AM radio. John struggles to remember whether it was a Chuck Berry number that Elvis performed, "Maybelline" or "Johnny B." that he first heard.

"I heard him on the radio for the very first time. And he sounded great to me. I'd never heard a voice like that before. He had a quality, Sam Phillips recognized it, too. He was a black man in a white man's body, you know, as far as the music.

"*It can't possibly be a white man. That's an interesting song ... *"

"And then when we saw pictures of him in the newspaper, in the local newspaper, or in the teen magazines or whatever, there's pictures of him, that's him. OK.

"So, I started paying real close attention and also about that time, again my friend Conway Twitty, bless his soul, came out with a song, "It's Only Make Believe." And I thought that was Elvis. And I remember every day when I'd come home from school at 3:15, about 3:20 or 3:25, KICK Radio ...

1520 on your AM dial!

... would play that song. I listened to it and I said, 'That's Elvis. That's a wonderful song. That's great.' And the DJ never said who it was. Until one day he slipped up and said, 'That's Conway Twitty, ladies and gentlemen.'

"And at that time, Conway was doing rock and roll, not country so much. And I learned how to play that. So, I became even more interested in voice quality. To me, Conway had a wonderful voice. Still to this day when I hear his recordings, I just love it. And his country things and even some of his early rock and roll things.

"And like I said, I thought Conway was Elvis, so I paid more attention to Elvis and when his records would come out, I'd go get the 45s, the old EP 45s, they had two songs on each side. Extended play. I'd get some of those, and I'd listen."

As far as Elvis the "sound" was concerned, John found something he enjoyed and appreciated in a new way. Voice quality ... especially, the black quality to the voice.

Finally, a local newscast showed a moving, speaking Elvis Presley to John for the first time.

"It was a news snippet of him on the Louisiana Hayride. They had some footage, and I saw that on TV. And there he was swinging and chopping that beautiful Martin D18 to pieces, you know? That was pretty cool. That sealed the deal. By seeing him and putting the voice and the person, the body together. That sealed it for me. I saw him do things that—I was only used to seeing people stand on a stage and sing with a microphone standing perfectly still. I hadn't seen anything like this, and my folks hadn't, either. In their day it was Frank Sinatra that the girls got all gooey about. I'd never seen anybody do what Elvis did in the early years. And I didn't think it was lewd and crude, I didn't get that kind of feeling at all. But then again that's where I was raised. There was nothing lewd and crude in my upbringing, and I didn't see that in Elvis.

"I thought it was exciting! Every move he made was with the music. His whole body's a rhythm player. I remember after watching those snippets from the Louisiana Hayride on the local TV, when I knew he was going to be on—later on the Sullivan Show, Dorsey Brothers and all that, and Jackie Gleason and Frank Sinatra show and all—I'd have my guitar ready to go and when he'd start,

I would play along—a lot better than he did!

"And seeing him, actually seeing him perform, not only just hearing him but seeing him perform, actually sealed the deal."

In Elvis, John's attention was drawn away from the guitar for the first time. John could obviously see the guitar and knew Mr. Presley was mistreating it. But he found he was more interested in the overall thing that Elvis was doing.

"My focus was not on guitar anymore. I was watching and hearing at the same time, this magnificent creature moving and singing at the same time. I didn't think you could do both at the same time because I hadn't been exposed to that kind of thing. So to me it was like a bolt of lightning hit me."

As much as John liked the sights and sounds of Elvis Presley, he did not approve of the way the young singer treated his beautiful Martin guitar.

"I had a high degree of respect for instruments. At that time there were no bands destroying instruments on stage, as we have seen in our lifetimes. But I had a high degree of respect for my instruments because, like I said earlier, I considered them to be a buddy, a friend, a very close companion, and I would never hurt my close companion. So that's all it was. He didn't have the same amount of respect for the instrument as I did, perhaps. But then again he wasn't trying to be a guitar player, either. He never was, really. It was just that I loved my guitar and I loved that old guitar of Mac's and the banjo of Mac's, and my respect for my instruments was my only gripe with Elvis."

In Elvis, John found one more reason to continue on his musical path. In subsequent years, he bought 45s: Jerry Lee Lewis, Little Richard, Ral Donner, Conway Twitty, the Kingston Trio, the Weavers, and Peter, Paul and Mary. Always, John enjoyed a wide variety of music.

"I like just about everything except this rap crap that's going on right now. I don't see that as music. And I don't mean this as a slur against the predominantly black genre there, the rap stuff. It's just, I don't care for it. I don't consider it music. I don't consider it music; they do. That's fine. They're making money at it—go ahead. Bob

Dylan was the first rapper, so these guys have not discovered anything new. But to me that's not music. The things I was buying was music. The things I listen to and use parts of in the music that I was doing. A certain chord or a certain riff or something."

John listened, appreciated and learned. However, again while very common today, most pop stars in those days did not write their own songs and John showed no initial interest in songwriting either.

"I wasn't interested in putting words down on paper and putting music to it. The Trio didn't even write their own stuff. And Peter, Paul and Mary didn't write their own stuff until a little later on, and then they wrote some things. I didn't think I really had that kind of talent. I did well in speech and dramatic art in high school."

Success in speech and drama did not spread to other areas of the curriculum. John much preferred playing music in Mac's music room to playing basketball in gym. And John's educated and academic parents did not appreciate the mediocrity of his other grades. Did John's parents give him a hard time about it?

"Yeah, they did, and with good reason. With good reason. You see, Dad's office was in the same building that our high school was. He was down on the very lower floor, and we were on the top three floors. It didn't look good when I came up on the list with Ds and Fs.

"You've got to do better than this. Why is this happening?"

"No, no, no, no, no, no. Look, I'm just not interested."

"But you have to be interested. You have to go to school. There's a law. You have to go to school. And it doesn't hurt to try to achieve like you have in music—you've become really good at what you do—it wouldn't hurt to put some effort into these classes that you must take."

"Math and science I had no love for whatsoever. Biology class, I hated it. But I liked Latin English. Mrs. Rice was the homeroom instructor on that. I loved anything that had to do with speech or music, poetry, things and translating the old Latin from the Roman and what have you. And I found that fascinating, and that led me to become interested in archeology, which I am to this day. And I had wonderful grades in English and history and Latin English and study hall—I did real good in study hall and recess. But I had no interest in anything else. Music really was all that I focused on. That and family."

— 2 —

By the eighth grade, John noticed three fellows a grade above him, who were also Kingston Trio fans and had even formed a little trio. They performed at an assembly in the gym singing songs of the Trio. John watched, realizing it was exactly what he wanted to do. He soon made friends with them after they heard him play at an assembly as a soloist.

"That was probably seventh grade, sixth grade maybe. Mac put on a Christmas thing where he had all the people in his choral groups that he would put together around all the classes for an assembly down in the gym, and he had me singing a lot of solo parts, and then he had me—I think it was 'Away in a Manger'—maybe I did on the guitar and sang to that. In front of the whole school. That was exciting for me. To be honest with you, yeah, of course I was scared. Maybe nervous anxiety would be better.

"I knew my guitar would never let me down. I had my best bud with me. And I felt very confident in what I was doing. I didn't have the confidence knowing whether they would like me or not. But I had every confidence in the world that I could pull this off."

The audience gave John his first standing ovation after that performance.

"And that was a rush, I'll have you know. There's a whole lot of difference between a standing ovation and playing someplace where there's the sound of one hand clapping.

"OK, I got this."

John reported this accomplishment to his parents.

"*That's wonderful, Johnny, that's wonderful. That's great. Keep on playing. Maybe you can do some more things like that.*"

John teamed with his father for his next big performance.

"The second big-time thing I did was with my Dad at the Kiwanis Minstrels. Dad heard a song on the Gateway Singers album that I had, a song called Dr. Freud. And as I mentioned, my dad was a psychologist. And Freud being the hotshot psychologist of all time, I guess, this song was just very clever. And Daddy loved it."

"Do you think you could learn how to play that, Johnny, on your guitar?"

"So, I learned it and wrote down the words and we sang it at home. And he belonged to Kiwanis, which is a service organization. And every year—they don't do it now, they can't do it—they held the Kiwanis Minstrels. And various people in Kiwanis—there was a group called the Singing Doctors—they were some doctors that sang—and they'd do little sketches on the stage at the Shrine Mosque, where Elvis performed. And Daddy had talked to the producer of that show.

"My son and I would like to be on the show. We can sing a song."

"And this little girl in between us, Mary Beth Evans, she was a dancer and she did her little act, and then:

"Dr. Richard Wilkinson and his son, John, doing Dr. Freud."

"And we came out on the stage and I kept my little guitar there, my little Silvertone, and we played the song we sang and everybody loved it. Singing with my daddy, that was big time. That was fun. That was fun. The thing about it at that time, nobody really thought about it, but the Minstrels—there was a lot of it that was blackface. And you can't get away with that now. You'd get in some real trouble from the NAACP or the ASPCA or the PTA or somebody, I don't know. But you can't do that no more. But it was all in good fun. There wasn't any kind of problem. We weren't making fun of anybody, it was just like the old W.C. Handy shows. And that's basically what these shows were. And we got to play this show, and that was a big moment for me to sing with my daddy. And we had matching sweaters—Mom got us matching sweaters—so we would look the same."

"I'd like to say how happy we are to be down here. It's a real honor for us to get a chance to appear on the Louisiana Hayride. We're gonna do a song for ya."

— ELVIS PRESLEY

John Wilkinson during his high school years.

CHAPTER 4

Rock and roll, and radio days

— 1 —

THE GOLDEN AGE OF ROCK AND ROLL, Chuck Berry, the Everly Brothers, Little Richard, Buddy Holly, Elvis Presley, Fats Domino, the Big Bopper ... John enjoyed all of it. And once again, he appreciated how music affected his female acquaintances.

"The girls in my high school, they'd have slumber parties, and us guys would go and visit them," John recalls. " Just having fun—no, I mean it—just having fun. We'd go over there and these girls would bring records, and they'd be playing them, dancing, and that's where we first got acquainted with hearing Buddy Holly.

"Buddy Holly came about '57 or '56, I can't remember. I do remember the very heavy rhythm patterns that he and his guys, the Crickets, were laying down. The girls were playing Buddy Holly music a lot, and some Elvis, but mostly Buddy Holly, and Conway Twitty. And this kid Buddy Holly, I hadn't heard at all on the radio, except "That'll be the Day" or something, you know.

"And I was really taken. I remember the girl who brought the album over; her name was Ann Rittershouse. And she's still one of my dearest, closest friends. Always loved Annie. Wonderful gal. We're still very close friends to this day. She had that Buddy Holly album. She brought this album, Buddy Holly, and all the songs were just terrific."

"Man, this is neat. That's not an acoustic guitar, either. That's not an acoustic guitar; it has to be an electric."

By that time, John had seen electric guitars being played by others. He'd seen Les Paul and Mary Ford, and admired them. He loves Les Paul as a pioneer in addition to a guitar player, having developed multi-track recording, echo effects, among many other innovations. In addition to Les Paul's guitar, John got an even closer look at an electric guitar in person.

"There was a fellow over in Central High School who was playing electric guitar. He had a little band and would play around town, at some of the pizza parlors that we would all go to. He had a four-piece band and he would play a Stratocaster. And so I had seen electric guitars. I'd never played one, but I'd seen them. And I thought they were an awful lot of trouble. I had my pal, my acoustic guitar, who would go anywhere and I wouldn't have to lug an amplifier with me. At that time, we didn't worry about amplifying acoustic guitars. The mic will pick that up, you know? Or we'll set up another mic for the acoustic guitar.

"Anyway, I noticed that Buddy Holly. That wasn't an acoustic guitar. And I remember asking Annie about that.

"*That's not an acoustic guitar, Annie. You know what my acoustic guitar sounds like. What the hell's that he's playing?*"

"*I think that's a Danelectro.*"

"*What?*"

"*I think that's a Danelectro. I think that's what my brother told me it was.*"

"*I don't know. I gotta find out.*"

"So I had a friend who worked at radio station KICK,

'*1320 on your AM radio dial, boys and girls!*'

"And I called this DJ, nice fellow, and asked him."

"*Roger, do you know what kind of guitar Buddy Holly's playing?*"

"*Yeah, it's a Stratocaster.*"

"*What?*"

"I wasn't familiar with Fender. I didn't know all these brand names then. I told Annie—I came back from phoning this girl's house who was having the slumber party.

"*Annie, that's a Fender Stratocaster. Tell Bill it's a Fender Stratocaster.*"

"He'll be interested in that."

"And the next day in school, she said:

"Bill knows what that is. He was thinking about buying one."

"When he does, I want to come to your house and I want to try to play it."

John found the cherry-red Fender Stratocaster to be quite foreign. In addition, it was not easy to play.

"I'd been playing acoustic for all those years, since I was five. Anyway, it felt very foreign to me. It sounded foreign to me. I tried some things that I was doing on acoustic guitar. It didn't sound the same. It sounded very foreign, very aggressive, I suppose. It wasn't friendly. I didn't get a warm, fuzzy feeling from holding that guitar and playing it.

"But Buddy Holly was playing it so it must be alright. But I got the feeling the thing was going to bite me or something. I just didn't get the warm friendly feeling. It didn't respond to my touch the way my acoustic would. That was my first experience with an electric guitar. And later on, I played some more down at the music store, just to try them, just to see what they were. But I never owned an electric guitar until many, many years later. I stayed with the acoustic."

Although Scotty Moore's Gibson ES-295 and L5, or Les Paul's namesake guitar were as prevalent as Buddy Holly's Strat, it was more than just Holly's guitar that struck John: Buddy's entire style affected him.

"It was Buddy's style of singing and the rhythms he was using, and he had a very rhythmic voice, too," John explains. "A hiccup kind of thing. Yes, that's the way to put it. And that coupled with his rhythm patterns on his Strat caught my attention. I was fascinated with Les Paul and the Les Paul/Mary Ford recordings, of course. I knew about Les Paul. I read up on him. Of course, we didn't have the Internet back then. But I ran into some people at KWTO radio station …

'560 on your AM radio dial, Springfield!'

… who knew Les Paul. And he came to town one time and he was at the radio station and I got to meet him. I actually got to meet Les Paul."

— 2 —

Although John does not recall the exact year, it was the late 1950s. Luckily, he had a connection at KWTO.

"Joe Slattery," John remembers. "He had a radio program in the mornings and he was playing country music. I met him for the first time, I think maybe when I went grocery shopping with mom and dad one day or something. He was in the grocery store. And dad had run into him at Kiwanis or one of the service organizations, whatever, working together perhaps. And he said, 'Hey, Joe, how are you doing?'

"I didn't know what the guy looked like. But I heard his voice.

"Mom, that's Joe Slattery. I just know it is."

"Well, yeah, it is. He and daddy are friends."

"Really? OK."

"And my dad, being the gentleman that he is, said,

"*Johnny, come over here a minute. Joe, I want you to meet my son John. John, this is Joe Slattery. You listen to his radio program.*"

"*Mr. Slattery, nice to meet you.*"

"*I understand you're quite a guitar player, John.*"

"*Well, I don't know. I love it.*"

"*I've heard good things about you. You ought to come out to the radio station sometime when Wayne Thompson's out there doing some recording and watch the fellows play.*"

"*I'll do that Mr. Slattery. Thank you.*"

"KWTO at that time was downtown but my dad took me down there one time. He dropped me off. He had some shopping to do or whatever for mom I guess. He dropped me off at the radio station and Mr. Slattery was there. And he said, 'You can call me Joe.' I never did. I never called him Joe. I always called him Mr. Slattery. He was an idol in a way to me, just as the singers I was listening to. Because he had this wonderful voice—he was on the radio after all."

Having never been to a radio station before, the various machines and microphones impressed John as he politely took it all in.

"They've got the sound board and the mixing board and all that," he says. "And all the dials and all the VU meters. They've come a long way since those VU meters now; it's all digital. But I was amazed looking at all this.

"Mr. Slattery, how do you work all this stuff by yourself?"

"I don't. I've got somebody to help me with all this."

"He had an assistant, of course, queue up the records and all this kind of thing. He showed me how that radio station worked. That was a big help to me later, too, learning how to work the mixing board and that was thanks to Joe Slattery."

Although he accepted Joe's invitation, John still didn't know quite what to expects on his visit. The workings of a radio station existed only in his imagination, based on impressions and information from listening to the radio and learning vaguely how a station functioned, as most people do. But how does it work?

"Is there a record player you put the needle on, and somehow it goes through the airwaves and lands in my radio at home?"

John courteously observed Wayne Carson and his band, his eyes carefully studying everything, from the workings of the station to the interaction of the band.

"So, Wayne Carson, who wrote 'The Letter,' a big hit for the Boxtops—was doing some demo tapes for some of the songs he had written. So I got to meet him. Mr. Slattery saw to that. And I watched him play. His guys that he had—he had a guitar player and a bass player and a piano player and a drummer. And I watched all of them play. I got to talking to Wayne Carson—and I did call him Wayne, there was no problem doing that because he and I were about the same age. He hadn't written 'The Letter' by then. That was later on. I called him Wayne.

"C'mon in here, John."

"And the tape machine was turned off, I thought, because if they ask you to come into the recording studio, you don't come in unless the light is off. And the light was off.

"John, come on in here for a minute."

"Alright, Wayne, I'll be right there."

"So I got out of the control booth and I went on into the studio and he introduced me to his band.

"I've been hearing that you're a guitar player, Johnny."

"I try to be, and I don't know if I'll ever do anything with it or not, but I love playing guitar."

"Why don't you take my guitar here and play something for us."

"OK."

"So I played and I can't remember—it was a Kingston Trio song that I did—and I can't remember what it was. It might have been 'Three Jolly Coachmen,' I don't know. Something that I sang, and I played the song and finished it. And, Wayne says, 'Playback.'

"What?"

"That's on tape, John."

"Uh, no, uh-uh, no, man. I didn't want to record anything. You told me to come in here and meet your guys, you know."

"Playback."

"And they played it back. And that was the first time I'd ever heard myself recorded. Damn, you're good, boy. Elvis was right. I was really kind of embarrassed at this moment because they were professionals, and I surely wasn't—or, they said I was, but I didn't realize that. And Mr. Slattery came in the studio:

"I knew it. John's—I told you I heard good things about you. You're good."

"Well, thank you, Mr. Slattery. I appreciate it."

Wayne and his boys applauding:

"John you're good. You're doing a good job. You're going to go places."

"Yeah, I'm going places alright. I'm going home. Thanks, fellas, I appreciate it. Glad to meet you. All the luck to you, Wayne. I hope your career goes real well. I'll be listening for you on the radio."

"I really didn't know what to expect. But with the help of Mr. Slattery, I learned. And I remember going back to school and telling these three fellows I finally teamed up with:

"I was at KWTO, '560 AM on your radio dial!' the other day. And Mr. Slattery down there—he's a friend of my dad's—and I met him and he showed me how a radio station worked. And I know how they will record when the groups come into town. They get in *this room and they've got microphones all over the place. They've got more microphones than you ever saw in your entire life, fellows. And they stand there and they sing and they play. And it goes from there to here and it comes out here, kind of thing, you know."*

"And they were excited about it. They thought it was pretty neat I had that experience."

As an adult, John acquired a reputation as a bit of a mystery man, mainly because he'd always been polite and respectful, not interjecting himself into any situation. If one watches the "That's the Way It Is" DVD, the early part in the rehearsal studio where Elvis is going over some of his numbers, John is seen but only his guitar is heard. Although he's clearly concentrating on the business of playing good guitar, it doesn't prevent him from smiling and enjoying Elvis's shenanigans. John's quiet confidence is a trait that surfaced even at this point as he was on the outside, observing, Wayne Carson and his band, not being too obtrusive.

"That was an early trait," John says. "I always would be on the peripheral and look in, just to see what's going on. And hence the mystery man title I got, the quiet one. Which has served me well. It wasn't something I tried to develop. It's just the way I am. Believe it or not, I really am kind of shy—sometimes. I wouldn't go in there and say, 'Give me that guitar. I want to sing and show you, I can beat all of you.' It wasn't that way at all. They asked me. So I was just another observer, watching and enjoying. Not only hearing Wayne sing and his group play, but what came out of that, where we went on the board and learning how a radio station worked. It was another learning process for me.

"But that experience meeting Mr. Slattery and that first experience of hearing myself played back—you know, we didn't have little tape recorders back in those days. They were using the big studio recorders.

"And shortly thereafter, my dad bought a Norelco analog tape reel-to-reel tape machine. And I'd set that up in my room. There was one microphone that came with the recorder. I'd play and I'd sing, record myself. Just for the fun of it. I'd play it back and think, 'That's pretty fun.'

"We used that recorder to record the Coachmen playing, my folk group from high school. All of a sudden, it was more locked into me, that music was everything to me. That this was the direction I had to go. I wasn't interested in nothing else. Music was just screaming at me like, 'This is your career!' This is what you gotta do. It wasn't that I was so impressed with my own recording or anything, but I enjoyed it. It was fun."

A similar experience befell a young Muddy Waters when Alan Lomax found him at Stovall Plantation, in Clarksdale, Mississippi, and recorded a collection of songs that are available as "The Complete Plantation Recordings." Muddy had no idea of his potential until he actually heard himself played back. John sold himself on himself because of how he sounded to himself.

"You sit at home and you're playing your guitar and singing," he explains. "You can hear yourself but of course there's a difference, hearing yourself play and sing when you're sitting there and hearing it played back to you. And you listen, 'Huh. Wonder if I could—maybe I should do that a half a key higher. Or a half a key lower or something. Or maybe I should use a capo and play a different fingering to get a different sound but in the same key kind of thing.'

"And you listen to that over and over again and again, another learning process. I was basically an outsider, I suppose. But not really an outsider because I knew my music. And I could stay up with pretty much everybody except Earl Scruggs. Ain't no way I could ever top Mr. Scruggs! Or Jerry Reed or anybody else who was playing guitar at the time, Red Foley.

"I remember my grandma, my mother's mom, taking me to the Ozark Jubilee, in Springfield. By the way, that was the first country music show ever broadcast live on TV. Even the Grand Ole Opry hadn't gone on TV. The Ozark Jubilee was broadcast live on ABC.

"And my grandma took me to see the Grand Ole Opry. Red Foley was performing that night. He was a big star in country music. He's been gone a long time. His daughter married Pat Boone. And through that I got to meet Pat and his family and all that, because I knew Mr. Foley. He lived up the street not too far from us. He was also the first person in town to have a 1955 white Continental Mark IV. Beautiful car. He's the only one in town who had one. I'd see him drive down our street on South Weller. I'd be in the front yard playing with my buddies or whatever. He'd wave.

"Hi, Mr. Foley."

He was always very nice to me. Halloween time, when we'd go knocking on the door, Mr. Foley would open door.

"*Hi, guys. Here's some candy bars,*" and all this kind of stuff.

"He was the first big country music star that I ever met. 'Old Shep' was his song. Which was to be a big song for Elvis. In fact, his debut song in high school.

"But Mr. Foley was the first big country music star I ever met. I didn't realize that country music was so big then. And through him I met Dolly. And Loretta, a bunch of other people, which was big time for me, because I was still basically a shy little kid out of Springfield, Missouri. I was a bigger kid then, but still I hadn't been exposed to the big time, if you will. The only real big time was Wayne Carson and in my mind's eye he's still a very viable artist. He hasn't done anything in years, I don't think. Wonderful voice. Good writer. And Mr. Foley, of course."

Still, for all his "big time," John knew Foley simply because he lived in the neighborhood.

"He was just a regular guy, lived in our neighborhood, little middle-class neighborhood, not too far from the university, walking distance for me and Daddy to—it would take it take us about 20 minutes to walk. Even in the snow it wasn't that bad. Sometimes, we got lucky and Mom would drive us to school. If it was really raining hard, of course. Mr. Foley just lived up the block until he moved to the Southern Hills area. Those two fellows were the first exposure I had to actually meeting nationally known singers. Except for Elvis."

Like being exposed to live music performed on television, John's grandmother exposed him to live music on a stage, which had an entirely new profound effect on the young man.

"I could have stayed home and watched the Ozark Jubilee on my little black-and-white TV," he explains. "But actually going into the auditorium and seeing these folks that I'd seen on TV actually playing in person. And my grandma, I don't know how she did it, but she had seats down on like the third row or something.

"So, I was right there, I could see all these greats playing. It was a real exciting time for me. I didn't get to go backstage or anything to see what was going on back there. I wasn't exposed to that until later on. But seeing the live performance really made the TV things I would see come alive more.

"Stereo back then was a speaker over here and a speaker over here. It was all mono, but the sound was out of two speakers—two massive huge things they had there at the Ozark Jubilee at the Jewell Theater, in Springfield."

— 3 —

It was when John was 15 or 16 that he got to meet Les Paul. Les Paul and his wife and performing partner, Mary Ford, an excellent guitarist herself, were in Springfield to do a concert.

"And they happened to be visiting Joe Slattery's radio station and Mr. Slattery kindly called the Wilkinson residence and asked for John.

"*Joe Slattery.*"

"*Hello, Mr. Slattery, what can I do for you?*"

"*You like guitars so much. You've heard of Les Paul, haven't you?*"

"*Absolutely. I've heard a lot of his recordings.*"

"*He's going to be doing a live thing here at the radio station with Mary Ford. Would you like to come down and see it?*"

"*Yeah, I'd love to. You betcha.*"

"*Well, come down. Tell the lady at the desk. I'll leave a note there that you're coming in, and she'll let you in.*"

John got to the station, excited. Hearing Les Paul in those days amazed and befuddled because although listeners knew it was only his and Mary's guitars, it somehow sounded like there were many guitars in their performance and John's inquisitive nature demanded that he discover the secret of those sounds because to him, Les Paul picked as fast as any banjo player he'd ever heard.

"So Mr. Slattery came and got me, and walked me into the control room, and Les Paul was there," John recalls.

"*Johnny, I want you to meet Les Paul. Les, this is John Wilkinson. He's a local guitar player.*"

John shook hands with him and Miss Ford. Les spoke.

"*You're a guitar player, huh?*"

"*Not like you, sir. I'd just love to know how you play so fast.*"

"*You know what? It's all done with smoke and mirrors.*"

Although it was the first time John had heard that expression, he instinctively understood its meaning.

"*I don't think so. I don't know what you're doing. Do you got two people playing the guitar or do you have two guitars?*"

"*No, I've got a little box here. Tape loop kind of thing.*"

"*I don't know what that is.*"

"*I'll show you.*"

Les took John into the studio area where the live broadcast was and he did some runs and riffs, recording a run, hitting a button, and playing a new run while the first run played continuously in a loop. Layer upon layer of guitar, with just one guitar player and a little box. It dazzled John. Not just the loop machine but Les Paul's speed on his signature Gibson guitar impressed and amazed with or without the box. And Les Paul was very nice and very friendly to John.

"*I've never seen anything like that before in my life, Mr. Paul.*"

"*You can call me Les.*"

"*OK, thank you, Les. I appreciate it.*"

"*You want to play it?*"

"*No, sir. No, I don't want to play that guitar. I tried playing an electric guitar before and I just don't feel comfortable with them. I just really don't.*"

"*One day you will. You watch.*"

They talked for a few more minutes. Chit-chat, a master and an up-and-comer with an insatiable greed for new musical knowledge, input and technique. John soon wondered if he was getting in the way.

"*You better get ready. They're going to be wanting you to set up and get your stuff ready to go here, I'm sure. Because once they turn on that red light, we're broadcasting, or they're broadcasting. I better get up there, but I am going to stay up and watch you play. You mind?*"

"No, no, sit right in there and listen."

"So I stayed for about an hour, and watched him do his magic as only Les Paul can do," John remembers. "And I was just fascinated. The techs that were working the board were having all kinds of adjustments set. "

"*Les, you've got to give me more high notes over there. I can't quite pick you up over here.*"

"So, Les would do some things way up there with the body of the guitar, you know? Incredible stuff. What a rush it was for me. And I left after about an hour. And I've never seen Les Paul again in person, nor have I run into him. But I remember him being just a real, real nice gentleman. He was very nice to me.

"He treated me almost—I want to say almost—like an equal.

"And then he showed me some things he was doing and his magic box. That's a big-time guitar player. Still, nobody can equal him, the things that he did and still does, when you listen to him. I was so impressed with him, that he was such a nice guy to me. Just a kid out of Springfield, Missouri. Just nobody, really. And that this big famous guitar player would talk to somebody like me the way he did.

"*Always keep your eyes on the dots, son. Know where you are at all times.*"

"He treated me like an equal. Of course, I wasn't and I'm not now. But I got the feeling that because he was such a gentleman, he just treated me beautifully. What an experience watching him play, actually."

— 4 —

"Those fellows," as John mentioned, who were a little older and had a folk band, and had impressed John so much in the school gym happened to be rehearsing in Mac's music room one day. Although John was in high school at this point, it was the same building as his elementary school and John still continued to visit Mac's music room and have his lunch down there: peanut butter and jelly sandwich, cottage cheese and Thermos of milk.

"Understand Greenwood was a laboratory school," John explains. "We had student teachers from the university who were studying to be teachers, educators. We had them, but I associated mostly with the class below me; dated the girls there. Our class was a real strange class, a real mixture of different types of folks. But these folk players were a grade above me. I never really talked to them. I remember talking to them after seeing them playing.

"*Fellows, that was really good. I really enjoyed that Kingston Trio, man. Yes, sir. That's my kind of music, too.*"

"The music room was down on the first floor, so I'd just go downstairs. And I didn't know, but these guys, that's where they rehearsed. I had no idea, but I was in the music room in his office, and I had my guitar—I brought my guitar to school. I was just in playing for a little time before I went back to class.

"And these guys—I heard the door opening into the classroom, but I didn't pay any attention to it. And I heard guitars start going and I hear them singing, recognizing they were the guys from the assembly.

"So, I peeped out and they saw me.

"*C'mon over.*"

"So I did. They were playing, and I started playing along with them and singing. They liked what I added.

"*Why don't you join our group? We're called the Coachmen, after the 'Three Jolly Coachmen' song, one of the Kingston Trio songs. We'll make it a quartet. It'll be the four of us.*"

"Bill Johnson had an old Gibson J 45. It was all beaten up, I mean really beaten up, but it had a wonderful sound. And the other two boys, Hadley Whitlock and Tom O'Brien, had four-string Kays, like Nick Reynolds used to play, a four-string Martin, in the Kingston Trio. They had four-stringers, four bangers, we called them. And they would play them. Bill was a pretty good guitar player. He had some rhythm patterns I really enjoyed hearing.

"Those two boys were just doing chords. But Bill had some flat-pick things he would do in the songs. He wasn't a finger-picker, though. He couldn't fingerpick at all. But I could, and when I started doing that kind of thing, adding in what I could do to what they were already doing, they really liked it.

"*You're a member of the Coachmen now.*"

"OK, good."

"So, we did a couple of assemblies together. Over in the administration building, there's a nice little theater in there that has a curtain and everything, and a stage. It's really nice. Padded seats. So we did a couple of assemblies over there. And at the time at the university, there were three guys who were going to college, of course much older than we, and they were called the Missourians. And they patterned themselves after the Kingston Trio, too. And it became a friendly rivalry after awhile between us and the Missourians.

"It was hard to tell which group was better, actually. In all honesty, I think we were. We had more *joie do vivre*, if you will. We were young. Young and stupid at the time, whatever. They were doing it to try to make extra money for their college work, or pizza and beer money or something, I don't know. But they were nice guys and they enjoyed listening to us, and by the same token we enjoyed listening to them. And occasionally, we'd get together and swap songs and play together or something. We never did a show together, but they were nice fellows.

"Anyway, the word started getting out around Springfield that the Coachmen from Greenwood are a great group, and people started calling for us to do backyard parties, that kind of thing. I think we did a church group, and supermarket openings, and that kind of thing, you know. Real big time in Springfield, and we just had a wonderful time. We played some pizza parlors, but mostly around Greenwood. And later on, down in Eureka Springs, Arkansas, which is not too far from Springfield. It's just basically across the border into Arkansas, down there, they have a thing called the Eureka Springs Folk Festival.

"And all these old players out of the hills would come down and they'd enter into the folk festival. There were guys down there playing zithers. I've got a wonderful recording of a fellow down there. And all he was ever called was Papa. And the album is 'Papa Plays the zither.' And the zither is an interesting instrument. It's a cross between a dulcimer and a harpsichord or something. It's played with fingers. There were other guitar players and singers, and banjo players and what have you. And we decided we should go down to that folk festival."

The Coachmen practiced seriously, utilizing the tape recorder and scrutinizing what they heard. And if it sounded good, they'd call it a keeper and keep the song. And if it didn't sound so good, they'd try to figure out what was wrong, or what the Trio did right. They tried to copy everything exactly, note for note, that the Kingston Trio did and they came pretty darned close. In short-sleeved solid green shirts, gray or black pants, and black penny loafers, the Coachmen took the stage, performing at the Eureka Springs Folk Festival twice, and getting a lot of notice. This was a festival not a competition, so the group enjoyed the experience without the pressure of winning or losing.

"It was just a festival, but you had to sign up, and you're group number 5, 3, 4 or 12 or whatever," John explains. "And you'd come out and you were allowed—you could do two or three songs, because they had a lot of these old guys from the hills coming down and they were doing traditional hill music, and we were pretty slick. We were city slickers, if you will. They weren't used to the kinds of things we were doing. But they liked us. We got a lot of applause and later on, way later on, Eureka Springs played a pretty big part in my growing up musically, too. But the Coachmen. That was my first experience with a group, and playing with a group and standing out as a more notable voice."

John found he enjoyed playing with a group in a way different from performing alone. He felt more "surrounded" by the music. He also enjoyed the companionship, musically and personally.

"Here's three other guys playing guitars, and I'm playing guitar or the banjo, whatever. I liked it. I liked the experience. Plus, I liked the guys. They were fun. We had shaving cream fights in the motel where we were staying in Eureka Springs. We were buddies. Great friends, and they still are to this day, friends of mine. But playing in a group—with that group—was later to serve me very well when I was in the New Christy Minstrels and the Goodtime Singers, and the Greenwood County Singers, the folk things. Invaluable experience working with those guys, because we really had fun playing."

And of course, there were spoils to go along with quality musical performance—as in the attention of the fair sex.

"Guitar players always get the girls," John states. "The ladies seemed to like us singing a lot. We wound up playing a lot of sorority parties and things.

"Sure, you want us to play? You betcha."

"And we actually made some money doing it. If we could get 20 bucks apiece, that was exciting times for high school kids. And if we played three times a week, or twice on the weekends or whatever, Friday night, Saturday, whatever, we could pick up a couple hundred bucks. That was big money for high school kids back then."

It is putting mildly that John's parents showed serious concern for the way his passion for music directly resulted in mediocre grades in school—or worse. Although his parents completely supported his passion, they did not approve of that passion at the expense of good grades and it bothered John.

"They were still being very cool about it," he says, "but I had a real bad feeling. I'm a real homebody. I like being home, or someplace where it feels like home. The house in Springfield, being with mom and dad and my buddies, and all the things that I'd come to love and know since I was a little bitty boy, I knew was going to come to an end.

"I was graduating out of high school, I was hoping. And I did, but by the hair of my chinny chin chin, just barely. And I knew that all of that was going to come to an end. What am I going to do? I don't want to leave Springfield. I don't want to leave Greenwood. Like I said, I never went to college. My dad helped me get applications for different colleges, and they even took me on a tour of a bunch of colleges in the Midwest, so I could see what other college campuses other than Southwest Missouri State looked like. Got brochures and programs and all that. I applied to I don't know how many colleges and, of course, they didn't want me. My grades. It's not that I was a bad person, my grades just sucked. But the University of Arkansas accepted my application, and I went down there. And I went to college to find out I didn't belong in college. I wasn't interested. I didn't know that. But it was party time."

The Coachmen, all a year older than John, had gone their own way the prior year. After they left, John kept playing as a single. He played the pizza parlors and city functions that would hire him to sing and play.

"I kept on playing by myself as a single and I wound up at the University of Arkansas," he recalls. "I shouldn't have ever even gone there. I started asking around, 'Who plays the guitar?'

"Well, there was a guy in the dorm who played the Stratocaster. Nice fellow. I can't think of his name now. Isn't that awful? Anyway, he was good on guitar and he was good on electric guitar—much better than I could ever be, at the time. I was acoustic, and he had an acoustic guitar, too. And then another fellow in the dorm played saxophone. And he was a real beatnik, I mean, a real beatnik. He looked like Maynard G. Krebs. Honestly, he had the beard, and the hair just like Maynard G., just like the Dobie Gillis show. And he had all the hip talk, he played saxophone and flute, I think. Slouched his way along, you know? Sort of like "Pig Pen" from the Snoopy comics, the Charlie Brown comics—you know when he'd gone by. So, this fellow who played Strat talked to him and we got together. And there was a guy named Wayne Sandy also in the same dorm who had lots of contacts there in the Fayetteville area, and he got us some jobs, and we were doing basically folk music."

Although the group focused on folk, a new sound intruded upon the status quo like a nuclear bomb—a group of four young men from Liverpool, England, with long hair and a completely unusual sound.

John performs with two of his rainy day friends.

CHAPTER 5

Discovered

— 1 —

*J*OHN HANDLED THE SINGING with his new friends. An acoustic fingerpicking singer, a beatnik horn player and a young master of the Stratocaster, played their songs amidst the changes in the air brought on by the Beatles. John recalls being in his dorm room in early 1964 when he heard them for the first time.

"I was in my dorm room," he remembers. "I had a little transistor radio that I bought down at one of those electronics stores down in town, I don't know. Anyway, I bought a little transistor radio to listen to and I remember having the radio on when I was skipping a class. It was ROTC I was skipping, actually. I didn't want to be in that. And the song came on, the singers imploring that they wanted to hold your hand.

"Oh, my God, what was that? That's wonderful! Listen to those rhythms."

"It just was so cool. So I called the radio station down there that was playing it. I introduced myself. I wasn't really known down there yet. I was just a hick out of the hills, wound up in Fayetteville.

"Who is that?"

"That's a group called the Beatles, sir."

"Can I buy a record?"

"I don't know if it's in the stores yet or not, but if you'd like, I'll make you a taped copy."

"Alright, thank you."

"So the radio station was just two blocks from my dorm where I was and I went down. He made a tape, cut it for me reel to reel, and I just played the hell out that. And one of the fellows, my roommate, had a reel-to-reel player, and he said I could use it. I listened to that over and over again.

"Man, this is really different."

"So, these fellows I hooked up with, Maynard G., and this Stratocaster player and myself, we then got an electric bass player. Nice fellow. I can't remember what his name is; it's been too long. He had a Fender Jazz bass. Real nice. And he played beautiful stuff. He was really very good.

"So, we incorporated the Beatles song with our folk things, and we did some Elvis, and we did some Conway. We started playing for dances and what have you at some of the clubs around town. And we stayed together that whole semester when I was there. And during that semester, there was a banjo player at the Sigma Nu house. He had a long-neck Vega Pete Seeger model. And he was good. He was a good frailer. He wasn't a three-finger picker, but he was a good flailer. He stopped me in the cafeteria one day.

"I'd like to talk to you."

"OK."

"We've been thinking about rushing you for Sigma Nu, to be a member of Sigma Nu fraternity."

"I don't know. I'm happy where I am."

"No, no, we'd like to have you."

"Well, the reason he wanted me is because he had a guitar player; he wanted to put a trio together. So they rushed me and I pledged Sigma Nu. I hated that experience. Because I wore my hair long—wing back, the whole thing—and I didn't fit in. I didn't have horned-rimmed glasses. I didn't wear suits. I was just a regular guy. But we had a trio. I can't even remember what we called ourselves anymore. But it was just something to pass the time. Every Saturday morning at the radio station down there they had a live show, and they had us come down and sing. It wasn't any big deal—just fun. And then I left the university—under a heavy cloud of suspicion (laughs). College wasn't for me. I got out of there."

— 2 —

One semester proved to John what he'd long suspected: He simply wasn't an academic. It didn't mean he wasn't intellectual nor did it mean he wasn't artistic; obviously, he was creative. But there's something about life itself on a university campus. One wakes, lives, eats and sleeps *at school*. The real world has a tendency to recede. John preferred that world and had no other wish but to fill that world with music. He returned home after that one semester—at first. His parents, though discouraged, were not surprised.

"They saw the handwriting on the wall because they'd gotten reports back," John recalls. "I wasn't a student. It just wasn't for me. Wasted a lot of my daddy's money, you know, doing that. But it was a good experience because I learned—what's that line? 'A man's got to know his limitations.' Thank you, Mr. Eastwood. All due respect to you, Mr. Eastwood, who by the way, is a very nice fellow."

John had a friend who lived up in Ames, Iowa. His plan: Go to Ames and get a job or something ... and play music when he could.

"So, I got on a bus and my friend met me at the bus station," John continues. "He took me over to this little hotel. Ames Hotel. I'll never forget it. And they had one room left, for $25 a week. It was all the way up to the top of the stairs. And there was two rooms up there—one on this side and one on the other. And it was a communal bathroom. Oh, what a dump! But it was neat. I had a window that looked out over a park, and it was nice."

John's friend, John Magnuson, was a big Dylan fan who also fingerpicked his guitar. The two of them finger-picked together beautifully and soon became good friends. They played various events around the nearby Iowa University campus.

"So I stayed there and my friend John Magnuson—I don't know whatever became of him, either—John and I started playing this duo. And that was the second time I ever saw the Kingston Trio. They were on the college circuit at the time, and they came to Ames, Iowa, and John had a line on some tickets."

"*I think I got two tickets lined up to go see the Trio. Would you be interested?*"

"Sure."

"At that time, I think the high-priced ticket was $10. So I saved up $10—I was going to buy some guitar strings, but I gave him the 10 bucks and we went and saw the Trio. That's when John Stewart was with the group. And I'd seen them live before when my parents had taken me to St. Louis the first time. They specifically took me to see my idols. We stayed in the same hotel as they were performing in and staying in.

"So, John and I went to see the Trio and we had a great time. And then John had had enough of college. He was like me! He was very—just not happening. And he was from Moline, Illinois. So, he called his folks:

"I'm getting out of here."

Magnuson read an ad for a dude ranch out in Montana seeking people to sing at the campfire every weekend. During the daytime, they could wrangle horses and perform ranch chores. Montana sounded very cool to a couple of 19-year old guitar pickers.

"So, we got on a bus and went out to Bozeman, Montana, and signed up. They hired us. They liked the way we sounded. We worked the whole summer up until about the middle of September, I guess. Everything from chopping wood to wrangling horses, bringing the horses down from the high country every day for the guests at the ranch to take their horseback rides.

"And on the weekends that we would have off, we'd drive into West Yellowstone, and there was a couple bars—there was a lot of bars there. We'd go in, we'd play, and they'd pay us 20 bucks apiece or 40 bucks apiece or something, I don't know. It was fun. And we made some money. Started getting cold in Montana right about that time. Time to get out of here! And my friend, we went to a junk yard, and there was a 1950 Studebaker there—that was running. And for 50 bucks, we bought that. 50 bucks. And John was a real good auto mechanic. He got it all fixed up, and it was running, and we drove that sucker to—well, it was Denver first, and we played at the cowboy bar, up there in Denver. And another place called the Bowling Pin, I think. It was a ratty bar."

The boys didn't have any real plan, just to head south to escape the coming winter. As Denver cooled that fall of 1964, the boys continued to migrate and somewhere along the way, realized they'd no clean clothes. Dirty laundry can lead to the first step of destiny.

"It was starting to get real rank in that old Studebaker," John laughs. "And we stopped at a washeteria—a laundramat—we called them a washeteria. There's no such word, I don't think, but that's what we called them. And at every laundramat you'd go to, there's always a cork board with ads up there. Dog for sale. Babysitting available for whatever. Well, there was a card up there.

"*If you're ever in McCook, Nebraska, and you can play guitar and sing, you'll make $10 a night and all the beer you can drink and all the pizza you can eat.*"

"Well, hell's bells. We'll do that."

"So we got a map, figured out where McCook, Nebraska, was, and John and I said almost simultaneously, 'Let's go there.' Why not? We had nothing to do, no prospects. We had no money really. I bet you we didn't have $100 between us.

"So, we wound up in McCook, Nebraska, and pulled up to that Pizza Hut. I'd taken that card off the board when we were in Denver. I walked in to the bartender—there was just beer and pizza in there.

"*Does this card mean anything to you, partner?*"

"*Yeah, as a matter of fact, my brother put that card up in Denver. Is that where you got it?*"

"*Yep.*"

"*Well, are you the guitar player?*"

"*Yeah, I play guitar. My buddy does, too, and we sing.*"

"*Where are your guitars?*"

"*They're out in the trunk.*"

"*Well, bring them in here and let me hear you.*"

"*OK, fine.*"

"So, we auditioned for the bartender, who turned out was the owner. So, we sang for him.

"*Yeah, yeah. You can start tonight.*"

"And it was a Thursday night, and there wasn't hardly anybody in. But we played, anyway. And we did three shows. And he liked us and he kept us on and we stayed there for, I don't know three months—something like that, I suppose. And then John got a draft notice, and he had to go back to Moline. So I stayed in McCook for a little while. And I was doing a single, and another guy who was a guitar player in town used to come in, Lonnie Cafferty. I just found out he passed away two years ago, on a phone call I got yesterday. Interesting. Wonderful—he did the very best version of 'White Lightening' I ever heard done. And big old 12-string and googly eyes, man, he was something. Big voice. He was wonderful.

"Anyway, we worked the Pizza Hut there for quite awhile. And as luck would have it, Randy Sparks, who was the owner of the New Christy Minstrels, he had a farm team for that group that was called the Back Porch Majority. That's where members of the Christys came from—well, he'd draw from the Back Porch Majority. And they were doing all the same songs, all the same things. Good program. They had been playing up in North Platte. There's a little school up there and they had been playing up there, and they'd come back to McCook and, as luck would have it, they wanted pizza and beer, so they had come in while I was playing. And I didn't know who they were. I'd heard of them, but I don't know who they were—I just saw these kids come in and sit down and order pizza, and a couple, three pitchers of beer, whatever. I was doing my job, singing.

"And after I finished my set—in fact it was my last set of the night—one of the guys came over.

"*Have you ever heard of the Back Porch Majority?*"

"*Yeah, I've heard of them. They're a farm team for the New Christy Minstrels.*"

"*You're right, and that's us.*"

"*Really!*"

"*C'mon over here.*"

"They were a seven-member folk group—five guys and two girls.

"*We like the way you play and sing. We think Mr. Sparks—Randy Sparks—would love to hear you play. Do you have a demo tape?*"

"Well, thanks again to Joe Slattery and KWTO. Before I had left, I'd gone in and made a demo tape, reel to reel, of every song I could think of, played and sang.

"I do have a tape. It's up in my room at the boarding house. I can go get it for you if you want."

"Yeah, c'mon back down."

"So I ran back out, got on the pizza delivery boy's bike and rode up to my room at the boarding house I was staying in, got my tape, came back.

"Here's my tape."

"Well, we'll take it. We're going back to Los Angeles tomorrow. We'll give it to Randy Sparks, and maybe he'd like to hear you sing. Maybe he can do something for you, I don't know."

They took the tape and a few weeks went by. John's excitement dimmed in the waiting. But all that worry was for nothing.

"And then the kid that I knew who worked at the dry-cleaning store was also a little bit of a guitar player. Randy, I guess, had been calling all over town trying to find me. And finally, somebody said to this fellow Bob Peterson,

"Do you know where John is?"

"Yeah, he's down there at the beer bar down by the railroad tracks."

"So, Bob comes running down there, and I was drinking red beers—beer and tomato juice.

"John, there's a phone call. A guy's trying to get a hold of you. A guy named Randy Sparks. You ever heard of him?"

"Oh, yeah, I've heard of him. You bet."

"Well, he wants to talk to you. You gotta come back with me up to the house, and he's going to call up there in a little bit."

"So we went up there. I had lunch with him or whatever. And the phone rang, and Bob picked it up.

"Hello? Yeah, he's here. Hang on."

"Hello? John Wilkinson here."

"This is Randy Sparks out here in Los Angeles. How are you?"

"Fine."

"I heard your tape. I really like what I hear. I'd like to have you *come out here in Los Angeles and work for me. I'll send you the bus ticket."*

"Groovy. Another damned bus ride. So he did, he sent me a bus ticket to Denver, and he'd also included a plane ticket from Denver to L.A. And I flew into L.A., and his houseboy picked me up took me over to the office. And I was discovered in McCook, Nebraska, I guess you might say. And that led me to bigger and better things in L.A."

*"I'm not runnin' Mr. Rowe down
but I just don't see that he should call those people idiots.
Because they're somebody's kids.
They're somebody's decent kids, probably that was raised
in a decent home. And he hadn't got any right
to call those kids idiots. If they wanna pay their money
to come out and jump around, and scream and yell,
it's their business. They'll grow up some day
and grow out of that. But while they're young,
let 'em have their fun."*

— Elvis Presley

Richard and Virginia Wilkinson, and their son John.

CHAPTER 6

Rainy Day Friends

— 1 —

END OF 1964, EARLY 1965 John arrived in Los Angeles. The 1960s were under way and John had never seen a city this big before. To this day, Los Angeles culture shocks any Midwestern transplant.

"It was really quite a thing for a country boy, a hillbilly, to see all these houses and buildings and what have you," John says. "I met Randy Sparks in person and he said he really enjoyed hearing me sing, and he told his houseboy to get me a room over at the Travelodge, not too far from Randy's club, which was called Ledbetters.

"You come up to the club tomorrow around noon, and we'll put you to work."

"OK."

"Well, I didn't realize what he meant at the time. I thought he meant playing and singing. But Randy had a formula that worked out real well. A little like Tom Sawyer, I suppose. He was building this club, remodeling the inside, anyway. And all the people he hired, the Back Porch Majority singers and the rest of the groups, were expected to help decorate the club. Put up the brick façade inside and the cork walls for the baffling for the sound, and all that. So I was put to work doing that, too."

It seems Mr. Sparks' artists doubled as construction workers.

"And Randy didn't pay anybody! He actually had a big house up in Brentwood that he bought specifically to house his entertainers. It was pretty neat. I didn't wind up there. I stayed in that motel for, I don't know, a good month, I guess. And then I got tired of that and I started looking for an apartment. And I found one not too far away from that motel. And then he started putting me on stage in his club. As a single. Just me and my guitar, singing all the songs that I did with the Coachmen and all the Kingston Trio stuff.

"Come to find out that what Randy was looking for was original material that he could steal and put his name on. It sounds like I'm badmouthing Randy Sparks. In a way I am. Because he found out that all you have to do with any song is change one word in the song and put your name on it and call it yours. So, much of the traditional folk songs that you would hear the Weavers do, and if you bought a Back Porch Majority or Christy Minstrels album, like 'On Top of Old Smokey,' or something like that, which is an old, old song, you know, your mom knows, and you see Randy Sparks on there.

"What he's done—somewhere along there he's changed a word, a single word, and put his name on it. I didn't have any original songs—except, well, I did have one, called 'The Wayfarer.' I sang that and he really liked that.

"That's a great song. I'd really like to have that. Maybe I can record you or give it to the Back Porch Majority and let them record it."

"OK."

"And I remember I had no knowledge of show business, the ins and outs of legalities and this, that and the other. All I knew was that it was fun to play guitar and sing. Because every time I played in Spingfield and down in Arkansas and all that, down in college town, the person who hired you paid you, and that's all there was to it. But Randy said:

"I'll give you $100 for that song."

"Well, I didn't have any money at the time."

"$100, sure, OK, fine."

"So, I took it and gave him a song. And it has never been recorded, by anybody. And it belongs to him. He's got his name on it. And one of the guys in the Back Porch heard (what happened).

"Did you give that song to Randy?"

"Yeah, I did, and he gave me a 100 bucks for it. How about that?"
"Well, you just lost that song. It's not yours anymore."
"What do you mean?"
"He'll put his name on that."

"And I guess he did make a demo himself and put his name on it. So I shouldn't have said it had never been recorded by anybody. But it never got released. It's in his lockbox of songs. It belongs to him. He copyrighted it and everything. But I stayed on with Randy maybe two, three, four months."

The practice of screwing artists out of compensation for their material came into existence as soon as music became a business. Countless black musicians especially were robbed of compensation for their songs. Usually, the white management received publishing royalties. Even the Beatles didn't receive appropriate compensation until 1969, not long before they parted. Randy did the same thing, if on a smaller scale.

Since the song did not make money for anyone, no real harm was done other than John lost his song—but not without learning his first lesson about the music business. Of course, he could always change a word and put his name right back on it. But then the buzz from his audience quickly took his mind from its wayfaring thoughts.

The audience liked him. He was the youngest performer there and he played Thursday, Friday and Saturday night gigs of eight- to 10-song sets.

"And I remember I had a little Epiphone 150, acoustic. And all the other guys were playing Martins and Gibsons and things, and I was thinking, 'Whoa.' I needed to do something about this, but I didn't for a long time, I kept that Epiphone. I loved that little guitar. Bought that in Springfield, as a matter of fact.

"For about four months I was with Randy. And then he said that he had a friend who owned a club in Scottsdale, Arizona, and they were looking for someone like me to work there with Dolan Ellis, who was one of the original members of the New Christy Minstrels. He had quit, and went to Arizona and he was—in fact, he had been made the official balladeer of Arizona by the governor down there.

"And Dolan and his bass player, Igor, had worked this club, and Igor was working as a single there and they wanted somebody else second billed to this guy. And Igor was really great. He played a stand-up bass like you would not believe. God, he was good. I don't know whatever became of him, but he was a nice guy. He was very nice to me. And actually after his set, I was supposed to come up, he would stay up and play bass for me against my songs, which I thought was very nice. No-extra-charge kind of thing. It was just a nice guy saying, 'Well, this kid's new. I think I'll just play a little bit of bass behind him.'

"So, I had a real good friendship with him and Dolan, Mr. Ellis—a nice fellow. So, I stayed there, I think it was three weeks at that club. And then I went back to California and worked some more with Randy, and then I moved on to other folk groups.

"I remember a night that a tall, lanky kid came in with the current haircut at the time—very collegiate looking. It was long, but it was very collegiate looking. I asked about him.

"*Who's that guy?*"

"*He plays 12-string in the group called Greenwood County Singers.*"

"I'd heard of the Greenwood County Singers. I heard some of their records on the radio. And after I'd finished one of my sets, I'd go down and go over and get a beer, and sit down and listen to the rest of the acts. It was talent night that night. So he had some of his people open the shows, and then people were auditioning for Randy.

"Fortunately, my tape did the audition for me, that the kids took back from McCook. I was sitting at the tables, sipping my beers, and this tall, lanky guy comes over and introduces himself.

"*Hi, my name is Bob Turner.*"

"*Nice to meet you, Mr. Turner. How are you?*"

"*No, it's Bob.*"

"*OK, Bob. Nice to meet you.*"

"*Our tenor singer in the Greenwoods is having to quit because he has to go into the army. And I like the way you played, and I think if I talk to the leader of the group, maybe you can join that group and get you out of here.*"

"I'd love to do that. I'd love to be in that group."

"So, he set it up with Carson Parks. C. Carson Parks was the leader, owner of that group. I don't know if that name means anything to you, C. Carson Parks, or not. But Carson wrote 'Something Stupid' and several other things that Frank Sinatra recorded. By the way, Carson's brother Van Dyke Parks is a wonderful studio musician in Los Angeles. He's been around a long time. Wonderful studio musician.

"Prior to that, however, Randy put me in the Back Porch Majority to fill in for a fellow who was sick. I didn't stay very long with the Back Porch. It was just a few days, maybe a week, when they were playing, I don't know, a bunch in California, way down in Nevada, Colorado, a couple of things, I think, then came back. I enjoyed playing with a big-name group. That was hot stuff for a kid right out of Springfield, Missouri. But then came the Greenwoods. I stayed with them through three albums, and eight hit singles. And that was pretty exciting.

"But again there was mismanagement in that group. I'll name names. What the hell? I don't care. Wally Brady was their manager and he stiffed us on a bunch of money, so we barely got paid, and never the amount we were supposed to get paid. But then that's showbiz sometimes. And you live and learn. I didn't know.

"The Greenwoods was a seven-piece folk group also, patterned after the Christy Minstrels, like everybody did. Les Baxter's Balladeers were the same kind of thing. I was never with the Balladeers, but I knew some people in it. I stayed with the Greenwoods until finally they broke up in 1966."

Before the group disbanded, however, Fate once again drew two musicians together: John Wilkinson and Elvis Presley.

— 2 —

In 1965, John was also working with two other guys as a duo, one or the other, whoever was available. They called themselves the Rainy Day Friends. Tom Drury and Dave Peel were John's alternating duo-mates.

"And we were playing the old Icehouse, in Pasadena," John recalls. "It was a wonderful folk club. People—all the big names of folk music played there. I did this sort of work when the Greenwoods weren't working.

"Dave and I were working the Icehouse and—there were two Icehouses, one in Pasadena and one in Glendale, and we played both of them. People like Gordon Lightfoot and John Stewart and others played at places like that. Wonderful folk clubs. And out of that, I met Tom Drury, who was looking for something to do also.

"And if you showed up on the weekends, you'd get a spot to play and maybe somebody would see you and say, 'I think I could use you,' or whatever. And through those connections and appearances, indeed people did see and hear. And then came the Goodtime Singers, Andy Williams' old group from his TV show. And they had broken up years prior, when Andy's show went off the air, that was the end of that group, they thought.

"One of the members, Lee Montgomery—talk about white-eyed soul. (Whistle) This guy had a voice. Oh, man. I think he's still alive and singing. And the bass player from the group, Johnny Horton—not the country star Johnny Horton, another guy—was wanting to maybe put the group back together again because a management company called Inarts—International Artists Productions—had bought the name and was looking to form the group again and put it back out on the road. Mostly probably on the Holiday Inn circuit where you play the bar, things in there, and some of the smaller clubs, but it, too, was a seven-piece group.

"And it just so happens that Lee and Johnny were in the audience one night when I was playing and also when Tom and I were playing as a duo, and said to me they didn't much care for Tom but they really liked me. And after the show got off stage, I went back to the dressing room area and this fellow walked in.

"*Hi, my name's Lee Montgomery.*"

"*Hello, Mr. Montgomery.*"

"*No, it's Lee. You're just a hick boy out of the hills, ain't ya?*"

"*The way you're talking to me, you are too! Yeah, I am. I'm* new to Los Angeles. I've been around here a few months, but I'm just now sort of getting rolling, getting people to want to book me and things."

"Well, you know what? We're trying to put together the Goodtime Singers again. Are you familiar with that group?"

"Yes, I am."

"We're looking to put together the group and only Johnny and I remain as members who want to be in the group. We're going to try to get two more girls to come in. And you'd fit right in, if you want to do it. I'll take you down to the management company tomorrow and sing some songs for them, and I'll sing some with you and we'll see what works."

"Good for me."

"So, they came by my old apartment I had there in Culver City and they took me down there to meet this guy, Irv Winehouse. I remember his name so well. Ugh. To this day it sends shivers up my back. You could tell the minute you met him, this guy ain't honest. This guy, no way he's honest. And he proved right what I thought later on.

"Lee and Johnny did indeed get other members to join. And it had been an acoustic group also. But Irv wanted us to go electric. Well, by that time, I played electric guitar. So he talked to Fender, the Fender Co., old Leo Fender, and had Fender sponsor us and so we all got guitars. I got a sunburst Strat. I asked for a Tele, but they didn't have any to pass out. Tom was in the group, and Tom got an old Jazzmaster.

"The Strat was a very nice guitar but the thing kept breaking strings. Not the way I was playing, of course. I was still finger-picking with metal finger picks and all that, and I was using light-gauge strings on the Strat—and they just didn't hold up. That's another story about the strings. The group, we got together, we rehearsed, Inarts Productions got us a rehearsal room not too far from the office, and we rehearsed every day from 10 in the morning until 5 at night. We put together three or four different shows, or sets, and they put us out on the road.

"Once again, some of these managers—this was the time I

learned Irv really was what I thought he was. We tried to get paid, and what they did was, the club owner or the event owner or producer or whatever would send the money to Inarts Productions and they would cut checks to us. And at this time we were in Santa Fe, New Mexico. He had air-mailed, or whatever, the fastest way was to get a package to us at that time. In '68, you know, you could send a letter for 10 cents or something I think, whatever it was. And we got these checks and I went to a local bank in Santa Fe.

"*Do you have ID, driver's license, something?*"

"I did. I had a passport and a driver's license at the time, so I showed that to him.

"*Alright, fine. We'll cash that for you.*"

"And whatever they did at that time, teletype maybe to a bank, and they got the action back.

"*There's no money in this account.*"

"*Well, wonder there that money went, son.*"

"It went into Irv's private banking account was where it was. So I called him on the phone.

"*Hey, these checks ain't no good, boy. They're bouncing. They won't cash them.*"

"*Oh, man, I'm sorry about that. I don't know why.*"

"*Well, I do.*"

"I went to see the president of the bank in Santa Fe and told him the story.

"*Now, what am I going to do about this?*"

"*Well, you call your manager and raise all kinds of hell about it.*"

"So I did. I called him, and I called him everything but a child of Christ, I'll tell you that. Because here we are away from home with no money, and we're looking to get paid. And this happens all the time. Still does, I'm sure, to some entertainers, especially young ones. You have no idea what to look forward to, or what to watch out for. But this bank president was real nice.

"*Where are you from?*"

"*Springfield, Missouri.*"

"*Do you have a bank account in Springfield, Missouri?*"

"*I have an old bank account I used to put my nickels and dimes in when I was a kid, and my father's well known in Springfield, and I do know the bank president of Union National Bank there."*

"Well, let me call that bank president and see what I can do."

"So a couple of minutes later he came back.

"I just spoke with the bank president of Union National Bank, and he knows you very well, and knows your family. And we'll work something here where I'll take that check and I'll make sure that it gets honored some way. But they're going to transfer that money to us, and I'll make sure that all you guys get paid."

"Which was pretty darned nice. He didn't know me. But thankfully, my reputation in Springfield was such, and my family's reputation was such that he would take that chance. And so we did get paid, but that just was just one of many times that Irv really played bad with us.

"We were all sitting around in one of the hotel rooms one time and were saying, and I remember very clearly saying, 'I've had enough of this. I'm not having fun anymore.'

"And music for me is fun. If I can't have fun with it, I don't want to do it. Anything. I said, 'I'm fixing to quit, you all, if we don't come up with something. I'm not the leader of the group, but I don't have to put up with this.'

"So we got back to L.A. and Irv had made all nice with us and had us up to his house for a barbeque up in the Valley or something, I don't know. I mellowed a little on that and figured, well, really I don't have anything else going on right now, I might as well stick with the group for a little while. Maybe it's a stepping stone to something else.

"And I stuck with them and the next thing he did, he replaced Johnny Horton who was also our arranger with one of his personal Yiddish friends. Morrie Yess was his name. And he was a wonderful classic guitar player, but he had no idea about—and at this time the funkadelic or psychadelic music was coming in. Jefferson Airplane, the San Francisco sound.

"And Fred Darian, Irv's partner, decided that we should start doing songs like that. Well, no. Don't want to do that. So he came over to rehearsal one day, this Fred Darian. By the way, he's the one who wrote that comedy song, 'Hey Mr. Custer, I Don't Want to Go.' It was a single, nationwide at one time. And he thought he was really hot that he had written that hit song for somebody, I can't remember who it was, Sheb Wooley or somebody that did it, I don't know.

"Anyway, Fred came in:

"*Alright, this is what we're going to do.*"

"Meaning, 'This is what *you're* going to do.'

"*We're going to—Morrie has written a couple of songs, and we're going to record them for the record album.*"

"We are? I'm thinking, 'Don't tell me what to do. Who are you? You don't play nothing. We're doing just fine with the music that we know.' We did all the old guitar/singer songs, plus Tom and I being folk artists also brought in things that we enjoyed doing.

"*Well, if you're not going to do what I want to do, you can just quit.*"

"That was enough for me.

"*I'm first. 'Bye!*"

"I packed up my guitar and took it down to the car, put it in the trunk. Took my amplifier, put that in the truck. And as the last thing said, 'Good-bye. See ya! It's been a slice. Good-bye!' And I left. Drove back home, where I was living, Culver City. And I'd no sooner gone through the door and the phone was ringing.

"Hello?"

"And it was Tom, my friend who was also in the group.

"*John, don't quit, man. C'mon.*"

"No, I ain't working for those people anymore. I don't have to. I'm good enough to get something on my own."

"But he talked me into doing one more show, and that was the Calgary Stampede up in Canada. Oh, two more. We did the Calavales County Frog Jump, made famous by Mark Twain, up in northern California. Those were fun. By that time, other members had left and they had replaced some of the other guys. So I came back to the group for two more shows.

"*That's it. I'll do two more shows and that's it. But I want my* money up front. *I don't know who's giving it to me, but before I stroke a single note on my guitar, I'm going to have money up front."*

"They wanted me bad enough because they said, 'OK.' And then after that second show I drove back to Los Angeles. I said, 'That's it, boys and girls. I love you all and it's been fun, but this is not my idea of having music as a career. I can do better than this. Not that you guys aren't good, but I can do better.'

"So I moved on from the Goodtime Singers. Then Tom finally quit, but by that time I'd hooked up with Dave Peel. He was a wonderful single artist himself. Now, don't get confused. There's two Dave Peels. There's a New York Dave Peel, who is a rocker. And then there's Dave Peel from Tennessee who's an acoustic folk picker. And we hooked up. We got along very well, and our voices blended very, very well. And we worked together for quite some time. How long, I can't remember. But toward the middle of 1968 is when I first go the call from Elvis."

But before getting that call, John and Elvis did indeed meet again in 1965, just as Elvis prophesized:

"Johnny, I just know we'll meet again."

— 3 —

In 1960s Los Angeles, a club called the Whiskey A-Go-Go, on Sunset Strip, became a legendary place where countless future superstars performed early in their careers, notably the Doors, Jefferson Airplane and Johnny Rivers. Especially in those days, it was a rock club, a psychedelic club, and John had played there a couple of times when they needed an opening act.

John played his folk music, harmlessly enough, which was still acceptable in those days at the Whiskey. One day in 1965, the Whiskey's manager called.

"John, this is Abe. Are you doing anything tonight?"

"No, I don't have anything."

Abe told John that Taj Mahal was scheduled to open for Jefferson Airplane that night but couldn't make it. Could John fill in?

John headed down to the club and while playing his set, noticed a VIP section of tables roped off from the rest of the seating area.

"Someone special must be coming to see the Airplane."

John played his set and headed back to his dressing room. As he freshened up after his set, a very large man stood in his doorway, startling him.

"Are you John Wilkinson?"

"Yes sir."

"Come with me."

John definitely did not like the looks of this fellow and immediately wondered if he was the wrong half of a couple whose woman he may have gotten too friendly with at some point.

"Can I pack up my guitar first?"

"We'll take care of that."

The big fellow led John from the dressing room to the VIP area, where Elvis Presley sat, there to see the Airplane with his friends.

"See, Johnny, I told you we'd meet again."

And so they did. And John accepted Elvis's invitation to party with his gang. The next day, John and Elvis parted ways—one last time—as long as Elvis lived.

*"The first time that I appeared on stage,
it scared me to death. I really didn't know what all the yelling
was about. I didn't realize that my body was moving.
It's a natural thing to me. So to the manager backstage
I said, 'What'd I do? What'd I do?'
And he said, 'Whatever it is, go back and do it again'."*

— Elvis Presley

The Good Time Singers.
John is top right.

CHAPTER 7

Recording for RCA and the late 1960s

— 1 —

As THE LATE 1960s UNFOLDED, John continued to live as a working musician. He didn't meet RCA's biggest recording star again during this period but he did become an RCA recording artist himself.

After the Bingham County Singers broke up, the bass player in the Freewoods, Rick Jarrard, got a producing job at RCA.

"He had told me while he was in the group that one day he'd like to record me," John recalls. "So, the time came when he was in a position with RCA to bring in a new artist. You might know Rick Jarrard produced Jose Feliciano and Jefferson Airplane's 'Surrealistic Pillow' album, among others. And he called me. This was in 1968.

"*How would you like to make some records for RCA?*"

"*Sounds good to me. I'd like to do that, I guess.*"

"*Well, I got some ideas of songs. You know who John Stewart is, don't you?*"

"*Yeah, as a matter of fact I do know who he is.*"

"He was the banjo player in the Kingston Trio after Dave Guard quit the group. That was the second incarnation of the Kingston Trio, if you will.

"And John Stewart had left the group in '67 and started his solo career. Well he and his wife-to-be, Buffy Ford, put out an album called 'Signals Through the Glass.' On that album, he had a song called, 'July, You're a Woman.' Rick had heard that.

"Are you familiar with this song?"

"Yeah, I got John's album right here. Been listening to it. Great song."

"He said that he thought we should do a cover record of that song and said I should do it. I said that's fine. So, he invited me down to the studios of RCA to do a demo, and see how it comes off.

"And it turned out the demo was what was released. It was like three takes, and Rick wanted me to sound like something, well, I don't know, it wasn't me. Had me all tightened up on the voice. But they released the record and it did very well for a first-time, unknown solo artist.

"He had me come back and do six more tunes, and they met with say moderate success."

In fact, "July, You're a Woman" actually charted. It tracked all over the United States, Australia and New Zealand, Japan and oversees in Europe. It got some notice the United States; it did well on the East Coast and Midwest, but not out west so much.

"Then Pat Boone came along. But during that time, say from '65 to '68, I was working as a single and traveling around doing the lounges at the Holiday Inns, the Royal Inns, that type of thing. At that time, the lounges would have single guitar players and singers, and that was perfect for me."

John got his gigs through a friend who also worked that circuit and he would recommended John to the powers-that-be who ran the entertainment circuit for those hotels. This got old quickly, however.

"After I finished a couple of those circuits, it got to be a real drag, a real drag."

For entertainment, John had several friends in L.A. and they'd sing together at parties and form a couple trios and duos, at the Ice Houses in L.A. and at some of the Santa Monica clubs. John still performed folk material as there was a call for it at that time.

"Then I met a fellow who played at a place called the Brass Bell, down in Santa Monica, it was a Beer Bar, great big old New Zealand guy, who called himself 'Pee-Wee,'" John says. "His name was Alan Roberg, and we got to be fast friends and he was just a giant of a man who played a hollow bodied Gretsch or Gibson electric, but like a Byrdland.

"I happened to be wandering down there one night when he was playing and when he took a break to come get a beer, I talked to him.

"I really enjoy what you're doing. It's fun."

"Are you a guitar player?"

"Yeah."

"Why don't you come up and pick with me?"

"It wasn't a high-class club but the crowds were great. So I started playing guitar with him and singing, and I think I did that many months, here and there, Saturday and Friday. We stayed very good friends and are to this day. And that was basically doing hit-and-miss gigs."

During the period before the RCA recordings, John hit what would really be the only lull in his musical career. As a fingerstyle picker who leaned toward folk and country, the psychedelic flower power era of pop music seemed a strange place in the city that gave the world The Doors.

"I felt kinda lost, if you want to know the truth. I didn't know what direction music was going to take and if it took a direction that I didn't feel like going along with, what was I going to do?

"I felt like all along, that folk music would have an audience. And I've been proven right. It still does in some places. I listened to the changes in music, I heard the psychedelic things come through, like Donovan, the Jefferson Airplane, and other groups like that. And I listened to their music and I liked most of it.

"I listened to all the music that I could. Some of my neighbors would go out and buy all the latest albums and I would borrow albums off them, and I'd play it, try to play along with it. But mostly, I didn't get the feel for what they were trying to do. I was still deeply embedded in the folk and country feel."

With this era being the peak of what could be termed a fashionable drug culture—meaning hallucinigenics were considered mind expanding and positive for people—John felt just as alienated by the drug culture as he was from that culture's music.

"To be honest, I didn't know that much about drugs," he explains. "When the Beatles came out, before that even, the Dave Clark Five, which was supposed to be an answer to the Beatles, there was talk in the trade magazines that they were doing pot or whatever. I had no experience with that when I was growing up in Springfield, so I didn't know, is that a mind-altering kind of thing? So, I had no idea what that meant until later when I ran into some people in the Hollywood community and recording industry and saw what they were doing. I had it offered to me and I said, 'No.'"

John doesn't let his preference not to turn on interfere with his appreciation for music when it works.

"The music's still good to this day. I don't know what my feelings were at that time. All I know is that I didn't need anything extra to come across on the stage this way. I could sell myself or my songs by myself, without a crutch, or I couldn't. If I couldn't, it was because I couldn't do it, it was my fault, not because I didn't take drugs.

"But I saw, I went to several concerts because of some friends, and the clubs, and I noticed that I could see the bands were wasted out of their heads. And I thought, 'That ain't no way to play. That is no way to play at all.' Your ears are supposed to be your best friend and you're supposed to use your own talent, your voice, whatever, to sell your song.

"But some of these clowns were exactly that. So I stopped going to these clubs and the concerts 'cause I didn't want to see that. I remember the days when you had your guitar, and you were a formidable force: You had the stage, and you could put that song out there and the audience would like it or not, that was their decision.

"But the '60s played hell with a lot of music and musicians, 'cause I knew it was drug induced, written under the influence of whatever it was: PCP, you name it. But I know now what it can do and I don't think it was in the positive at all. Never saw a musician yet high on drugs who could pull off his full potential to the audience.

"My feeling about the audiences is that the people came from a long way away maybe, coming down from San Francisco or Los Angeles, and they had to get a hotel room for a couple nights, food, whatever, so it cost those people a lot of money to come to see me and I didn't want them to go home and say, 'God, I'm sorry I went.' I never wanted any audience member to go home and say they were sorry that they went. I don't need that kind of reputation."

— 2 —

Despite the hindsight advantage of being able to label much of the music of the late 1960s as "drug music," it wasn't all electric Jell-O. In fact, there still existed a large folk-flavored audience as the mid-1960s saw the first of the folk festivals, which can also be credited with rediscovering many "lost" country blues greats such as Skip James, Son House, Mississippi John Hurt, Bukka White and revitalized the careers of Muddy Waters and John Lee Hooker. These are the fathers of American pop music.

Of course, Bob Dylan, whose "importance" is diminished due to changin' times, was a potent force in the 1960s and influence not only as a singer but as a songwriter, whose songs gave hits to the Byrds, Jimi Hendrix, and Peter, Paul and Mary. The Byrds are historically credited with marrying the Beatles to Dylan, electric guitars to acoustic songwriting.

John easily noticed the folk end of the spectrum of what was then fashionable, and it included former Byrds member David Crosby's group of harmonizing mellowness.

"Stephen (Stills) is a wonderful guitarist and writer, all of them (were in Crosby, Stills, Nash and Young)," John says. "I thought the Byrds, CSN&Y, I thought, 'It's coming back to the folk thing.' It was folk-rock, but it was more the way I was looking for music to go, and it did for awhile."

Music historians look at Dylan's country-fried "Nashville Skyline," as a kind of response to all the excesses of the psychedelic music at the time.

"Dylan, what a character. I know Bob real well. I used to sneak off to New York every once in a while and go to the (Greenwich) Village where he had his apartment, and Judy Collins had hers, and

Joan Baez hers. We'd get together and I became good friends with all of them.

"And of course Bob Dylan, was the original rapper. 'Girl from the North Country' although there was a melody to the music, the rhythm to the words was like rap—and it was positive."

John enjoyed observing the evolution of music during those fertile years.

"I listened to the changes, and was fascinated by the way music was able to change. The musicians found a certain formula, and it caught on. Now most musicians, performers, when they find a hook, or something that really works, that's what you want to stay with.

"The Beach Boys and others of their yoke, began to notice that they needed to make a change to stay viable rather than keep doing the same thing. So the changes that they made, I was fascinated by.

"They began with acoustic things, and not so much the beach, California sound—Dick Dale stayed as long as he could with that sound—and so the changes I thought were positive. But I thought well how that's going to go over, you know, by record sales. *Hollywood Reporter* and *Billboard* to see if their music kept going.

"Now there's one group, the Modern Folk Quartet, Cyrus Faryar was the leader in that group, and a good friend. Jimmy Yester is in that group, too. Originally, they came out, right about the time all the other folk groups did, but they had a different sound. They were using jazz harmonies, dissonance, things like that. It was fascinating, that they were using acoustic instruments.

"Tadd Delts was playing the banjo. It's really amazing stuff. Then when I first got out to California, some people that I met at LeadBetters, when I was working for Randy Sparks, one Saturday invited me out with them.

"*We're leaving to go see the Modern Folk Quartet, do you know them?*"

"*Well, if it's the Modern Folk Quartet, I'd love to see them.*"

"'Cause I thought they'd be doing the same thing (they'd been doing) that I'd loved them for in the first place. But they weren't, they changed. They did a song that I guess was a hit for them called 'Nighttime Girl.' More along the lines of psychedelia, but it was good. I watched that group that I had a lot of respect for go into something different with marvelous harmonies. I liked most of the changes I heard."

As a guitar player, John also enjoyed observing and listening to the emerging "guitar heroes" of the era, such as Eric Clapton, Jimmy Page and Jeff Beck, all Brits.

"Eric and I are good friends, and I love Eric Clapton's playing," John says. "There's not a style going that he can't play. Eric is an incredible player. He keeps on, and everything he comes out with, it's new.

"And now, Page, Jimmy Page, I will admit that he's probably a great guitar player, but his style I don't particularly care for. It's just a style that many other people like. And it's just the same thing with Hendrix, it seemed to me these two guys had a style of playing: loud and louder. It's not to take away from the talent they had on the fretboard but it was not something I enjoyed.

"Whereas Clapton could play whatever, acoustic and electric. Jeff Beck, well I just couldn't get into his playing. But what he played was technically great but I didn't feel any warmth."

John also had mixed reviews about some of the other more famous bands of the decade.

"I can't stand the Stones and I never could. I didn't get along with them personally, and that's OK because they couldn't stand me either. I know they loved Elvis but they put him down quite a lot. They always billed themselves as the 'Greatest Rock 'n' Roll Band'—I don't think so.

"The Doors I thought they had—I enjoyed some of the stuff they did. But the Rolling Stones, who knew, they're going strong today. And they're still doing the same thing. I never got into their music. To me, it wasn't music. It was noise. Maybe it's because I love playing music together; the melody line, I like to think in terms of where can we put the third for harmony and where can we get a story out.

"Now, I'm sure Mick (Jagger) would tell you all their songs have a story. Well, they probably do, in their minds' eyes. But I don't really want to say too many bad things about them because they're successful. I know there are a few people who agree with me about the Stones but for the most part, people say they are something else. Well, I agree, they are something else, though I'm not sure what."

What about Santana?

"Oh, my lord. Carlos was then and is now a spectacular guitarist. And Carlos is a real guy. He's someone you can talk to. I could say:

"Carlos, my name's John Wilkinson and I played guitar for such and such, and I really like your music."

"C'mere John, pull up a seat and have a brew."

"He wouldn't go on and on about himself, like Mick. Carlos really feels his music. I'm glad he's getting more recognition."

— 3 —

Along with changing styles of music during the 1960s, the Beatles started a trend that continues to this day: pop musicians writing their own material. Before the Beatles, aside from a few artists such as Buddy Holly, Roy Orbison or Little Richard, most artists performed songs written by professional songwriters. John did not write songs, he interpreted songs written by others, an art form all its own.

"I like to give a good interpretation of a song and turn it the way I want to do it," John explains. "For instance, Conway Twitty made a radio scene with 'It's Only Make Believe.' Now, there is a song I know I'd like to do. But there's a high part in there where I know I'd never hit but I can still do the song and get around that high part by doing something else with my voice.

"So, you take a song that you like, and I sit beside the radio every afternoon and wait for that song to come on and write down those words. The next day, I'd listen and figure out progressions from there, whether it was D or whatever. And then I'd start singing the song like he would, did, and then it would evolve naturally into my style.

"I even did a finger-picking version of it. Not recorded but used to do it when I went out there myself. You take a song, and if you like it when you hear it, think it's something you're capable of doing, write it down and take your own style and see if it fits your style. If it doesn't, if you can't fingerpick it, in my case, I better leave that alone. It was done better by Conway or whoever and I think I'll just leave that one alone and leave it on my record player."

As far as John's brief recording career for RCA went, he wasn't given the opportunity to "interpret" 'July, You're a Woman,' merely to record it as Rick Jarrard wanted it.

"They gave me the demo records to take home, and I'd listen to them and I'd try to put my own style to them. And on the songs Rick Jarrard picked for me, I liked them, but he wanted them to be in the same rhythm and same tempo and all that as the original artist. I didn't want to do that. I wanted to, it was my idea since I was new, to do it the way I would do it. But that was not to be. But I enjoyed all the songs he picked for me."

Soon enough, it would all be moot as Mr. Presley was assembling his live performance machine while John made his sides at RCA. The call to join the TCB Band was somewhat of an interruption to John's solo recording career but John suspects it was not a bad one.

"The call from Elvis really interrupted that career if there was one to be had at all," he recalls. "Because to be very honest, I feel I was used to be a write-off for RCA. They will do that, or a lot of companies will do that. They will take a new artist and put some money behind it, record you, maybe you'll get lucky and get a hit, maybe you won't, but they take the whole thing and write it off. So they didn't promote it."

For the record company, it's win-win either way: If it's a hit, they win, and if it doesn't, they can write it off and they still win.

"So they wrote me off. So, when Elvis came around, onstage when he was in Las Vegas he would say, 'This guy makes records for RCA (meaning John).' He heard all my records, he had copies of them. I don't think there was a career in recording for RCA with me. That doesn't mean anyone reading this might not have a shot at RCA or Sony or whatever. I think to be very honest with you, I wasn't ready. I was very young, 21, 22, wasn't ready emotionally or professionally trying to get hit records. I was more interested in performing live. I love the reaction of the crowds or whoever was in the club, even a crowd of two people."

Unfortunately, the RCA recordings did not boost John's career at that time nor did it give him additional enthusiasm. He remained frustrated, doing the club circuit.

"I'm not a writer, I'm a good interpreter. I take someone else's song and do something really nice with it. I'm not a writer. I did try writing a couple of things, I wrote the one thing right out of high school that Randy Sparks stole. But I was concentrating on guitar, banjo and voice, and the songs I had at the time to present to my audiences. The RCA, while exciting, as not many knew anyone who had a recording contract with RCA, that was a big deal and I wish it'd worked out differently but it didn't and that's OK. I moved on from there."

Indeed, John was about to move on to the very pinnacle of performance.

John's Singles

"The only trouble with 'July You're a Woman,' is that Rick Jarrard, the record producer, tried to make me sound like something I didn't want to sound like. He tried to make me tighten my throat to sing, and I would prefer to let my words flow.

"So, on 'July You're a Woman,' although it did very well until Pat killed it, it's not what I wanted it to turn out to be. I'm still proud of it because it was my first record in an RCA contract, my gosh.

"The other songs I did, one that I really liked that I was hoping would be the side they would release, was 'You Got Nothing to be Ashamed Of.' Wonderful thing."

"On rhythm guitar, he makes records for RCA Victor, his name is John Wilkinson."

— Elvis Presley introducing John onstage, February 23, 1970

John plays banjo during his folk era.

CHAPTER 8

All the King's Men

— 1 —

ONE DAY, JOHN GOT A PHONE CALL.

"I had three other guys who played behind me, friends," John explains. "And I remembered that I was sitting at home. I had a nice little house in North Hollywood. It was a Saturday, it was raining, my car was in the shop, and I was sitting there half-drunk on red wine watching 'Ozzie and Harriet' reruns on a black-and-white TV.

"So, the phone rings. And you have to understand all my buddies, all my friends I'd made knew I was an Elvis fan. And sometimes those guys would call and try to sound like Elvis just to try to fool me. (They knew) when one of his records came out, you know, I'd be the first one in line at the store to go get one or whatever. So this particular Saturday, the phone rang. I picked it up.

"Hello?"

"Hello, John? This is Elvis Presley."

"Yeah sure!"

John slammed the receiver to its cradle, outraged that his friends still played this juvenile prank on him. The phone rang again.

"*Dammit, John, this is Elvis, don't you hang up on me!*"

The day quickly turned surreal as Elvis told John a car would pick him up and to bring his guitar. And for the third time, John met Elvis Presley. But this time, they would not part. Elvis decided to go back to live performance. John thought that was great. Elvis burned out on his career of making fun if inconsequential (though profitable) films and after the success of the '68 "Comeback Special," decided to get back to performing music.

James Burton, who'd played on John's RCA recordings, helped bring John into the fold. Elvis liked John's playing. He wanted John to play rhythm guitar in his stage band. James would play lead. He held out his hand.

"I don't have my contract with me John. Will this do?"

They shook hands and little did either know that they would be bandmates until Elvis passed, without John missing a single show, of nearly 1,100 concerts.

— 2 —

"Is this really happening?"

Having been an Elvis fan since nine, walking into the rehearsal hall at ABC, was an I-can't-believe-this-is-happening-this-is-a-dream-come-true moment for John.

"How many kids my age can say their childhood dream has come true? Mine did. And being in the presence of all those fabulous studio musicians, James, Jerry, Ronnie, all those wonderful studio musicians, having seen their names on backs of albums—they played for everybody, not just Elvis. I was in the presence of greatness.

"These musicians were far and above professionally what I was, and had been at it a lot longer. James could outplay everyone. I knew that and I wasn't intimidated by it because I knew what I had to offer. Elvis liked what I did, which is why he hired me.

"Having Elvis walk in and say, 'Let's do That's All right, Mama,' and he's at the microphone, and he's singing and he's moving.

"I'm like, 'I remember watching you on TV on the Ed Sullivan Show. You were moving but they wouldn't show you. Jackie Gleason you moved but I didn't catch it.'

"He was feeling the music and he liked what we were doing.

"You guys really groove good together."

"We all looked at each other.

"*Well, maybe we do. And if it works good for you, boss, it works for us.*"

"I was a bit in awe, not only because of Elvis but because of these fabulous musicians who agreed to work with one another and Elvis."

John's initial presumption was that Elvis was going to put together a "greatest hits" package of his most famous songs. He was pleasantly surprised that Elvis also wanted to evolve.

"When we first started, I thought OK, he's gonna do the same things as when first came out, 'Hound Dog,' 'I Was the One,' 'Heartbreak Hotel' and some movie songs. He did 'Can't Help Falling in Love' from 'Blue Hawaii,' which is good.

"At first, he didn't say what he wanted to do. He'd do the old things to get warmed up. I wondered if we were really warming up or rehearsing what we'll do on the road. But I also remembered something he said.

"*I'm not going to forever do 'Heartbreak Hotel' and 'Hound Dog.' I'm not going to do it. I'm gonna get some new things for you guys to learn.*"

"We were like, all right, good, because you can go beyond 'Hound Dog,' Elvis, you can go a long way beyond that. Not that there's anything wrong with those but he had such a voice and such a talent and we all knew, and we talked about it later: He's gonna do something and he did, and the new songs that came out in 'That's the Way it Is' were dynamite songs, and I think it surprised the audience because they were expecting what he used to do.

"And they would have loved him for it but all this new material like 'How the Web Was Woven' sticks in my mind, great song. And 'It's Midnight,' and as we moved on and he wanted to expand his voice more, things like 'An American Trilogy' and 'My Boy,' all those big orchestra songs that showed the power of his voice, 'You Gave Me a Mountain'—then we knew it was going to be a resurgence of his career, the reemergence of Elvis, not a comeback because he never left ... as far as I or the fans were concerned.

"This was a new area for him to explore, songs and lyrics that had some meaning, something he could get hold of and turn into gold. I don't think he cared so much if they made the radio or not but he wanted to say, 'See, I have some wonderful new songs here and I'm really liking this. This is what we're going to do.'

"Well, aside from a couple of those songs after 'That's The Way it Is,' we never did any of them anymore but that was because of the audiences. They wanted to hear something else so eventually he started putting in those big songs he wanted to do, big orchestra, singers, that sort of thing.

"At the beginning, I don't think any of us knew what he wanted to do. I'm not even sure he knew what he wanted to do. We knew he'd had it with those movies even though he walked away with a cool million in his pocket every time he made one.

"He wanted to be back out in front of an audience because that's where he belonged and he wanted to show them their trust was well placed.

"*I can do something other than 'Hound Dog,' something like this. I hope you like this.*"

"And that was important to him. For us, it was important, too, because those old things got old in a hurry. Every night but he'd throw them in because that's what the audience expected. They wanted to hear 'Hound Dog.'"

This issue was solved simply by putting a string of the old hits in a medley, to sort of get them out of the way but without discounting the audience's desire to hear them.

"So, he'd do 'All Shook Up,' 'Hound Dog,' 'Heartbreak Hotel,' just fast versions, a verse apiece, have fun with them and laugh at them or whatever. Put them in a medley, get them the hell out of the way so we could move on to something else."

"Dammit, John, this is Elvis, don't you hang up on me!"
— ELVIS PRESLEY

Another Elvis wannabe? John, age 10.

AT upper right Miss Meredith Evans, who will be featured in a song and dance act, is pictured with Dr. Richard Wilkinson and son, John, who will sing a modern ballad duo, with guitar accompaniment.

COMPLIMENTS
Rolph Thieme

John, 11, and Dad, backstage at the Kiwanis Minstrels, held at the Shrine Mosque.

John, the banjo-pickin' fool, 1968.

John in his Las Vegas apartment with a Martin D-28S, circa 1971.

Onstage, Elvis jokes with the audience wearing a two-piece suit for the first time as the smiling Sweet Inspirations, John and JD Sumner looking on.

John watching and James Burton concentrating with Elvis singing, "God I hope these pants don't split on me!"

Dave Peel and John in Lincoln, Neb., circa 1972 during a break from the TCB Band.

John and Tom Drury play for a USO club, Nellis Air Force Base, in Nevada.

John and Dave Peel perform in Bear Valley, Calif.

John and his Martin D-28S at Mom's house in Springfield.

John, after just finishing a show with Elvis at Chicago Stadium, joins Dave Peel at Patrick's Pub for some additional performance time.

John and Dan Durako, bass player for his group with Dave Peel, the Rainy Day Friends, posing in Balboa Park, San Diego.

John's first time onstage after his stroke in Mol, Belgium, April, 1999.

John signs an autograph for a fan.

With Peter Verbruggen at his museum in Mol, Belgium. Peter has all of John's stage outfits.

Mr. Murphy, John's famous Gibson Crest, played around 1,200 shows with John and Elvis, on display at Peter's home Mol, Belgium.

"*Man, I was tame compared to what they do now.
Are you kidding? I didn't do anything but just jiggle.*"

— Elvis Presley

CHAPTER 9

Taking care of business

— 1 —

THE NOW-FORMED, SOON-TO-BE-CHRISTENED TCB Band began to know one another. The prospect of playing in Elvis Presley's stage band excited all of them. John was the baby of the group at 23—and this was a huge break in his career. The musicians shared their excitement with each other as they became more familiar.

"We were all just really stoked about the whole thing," John recalls. "Because this was a big move for all of us, although James had the reputation of working with some very big names prior to Elvis—but nobody as big as Elvis. Anyway, we talked. Ronny was really the leader in talking, because he was responsible for putting the kick in.

"Alright, now, does anybody have any questions about what we're going to do on, 'I Got a Woman?'"

"Don't think so, Ron. Think we got it. Why, did you hear something you didn't like or something that you want to change?"

"No, no, I just wanted to know how you guys were feeling about the music we were going to do tonight or tomorrow."

The new band mates talked musically about some of the people they'd worked for in the past. They all had good stories.

"Glen D. worked for Buddy Holly, but he wasn't a member of the Crickets that would work with Buddy. Waylon Jennings played bass for Buddy, you know, and the only reason he was alive was because he gave up his seat on the plane to take the bus to the next gate. That's the only reason Waylon wasn't killed in that crash, too.

"Glen D. had wonderful stories about the people he'd played for, and James, too, also had wonderful stories to tell about a lot of the people he'd worked for. He'd played for just about everybody's album at the time. And Ronny, of course, had played drums for a lot of people. Larry Muhoberac, the piano player, had played for a lot of people. So, I really got a kick out of listening to them saying stuff like,

"Do you remember Ella Fitzgerald? Remember that gig we did with her, and she wanted some soft drum things? I had to use brushes all night? And, Larry, you remember doing those high things on the piano for her to feed off of when she'd do her scat talk?"

"Yeah, yeah. That was a lot fun, wasn't it?"

"And I'd listen to these guys, because they were far and above me in experience. I hadn't worked with any of those notable names at the time. Later on, I played for a lot of people in sessions and on the road."

The songs tried and kept or discarded eventually came down to a set Elvis liked. John, for his part, completely approved of Elvis's choices as the perfect representation of what he was earlier and where he'd come to in 1969.

"There was all the oldies, of course, and then some of the older stuff that he really didn't do very much on stage, even in the early years, like 'I Got a Woman.' It was an encapsulation of the complete Elvis Presley. What he used to do, where he'd come to and what he would do later, those first shows at the International Hotel."

As the opening night approached, with the band booked into the International Hotel, in Las Vegas (now the Las Vegas Hilton), Elvis showed signs of nervousness, not just because he hadn't played before a live audience in many years and the world had changed since then but he felt a bit jinxed by Las Vegas itself.

"In 1956, the Colonel booked him into the New Frontier Hotel, in Las Vegas," John explains. "He thought that Elvis was ready for Vegas, and he was. But Vegas wasn't ready for him. He wasn't Dean Martin or Frank Sinatra singing the crooning songs, he was this wild kid dancing around up there, shaking his leg, and singing things that Vegas just wasn't ready for."

In addition, his 1956 fans were nowhere in sight at the Vegas venues: It was all grownups in the audience.

"There weren't really fans in the audience and they didn't know what to make of him," John adds. "And those guys at the Grand 'Ole Opry didn't know what to make of him and they kicked him out. So, they had to cut that gig at the New Frontier a little short. He didn't finish out the gig. And he was very discouraged about that. He called us into his dressing room opening night."

"Guys, I was here once before—not in this hotel—but I was here in Vegas before, and they'd liked to run me out of town on a rail. I hope these folks like me. We've worked really hard, guys, and I really hope they like me."

"Don't worry about a thing. You'll be fine. You're wonderful. You're really terrific."

"He wasn't looking for compliments or anything. He wasn't fishing for that kind of thing. He just wanted reassurance, not only from his close buddies that were his bodyguards but from his buddies who were his band who make the music for him.

"Because the music stops, and he's out there by himself. And the Sweet Inspirations were very supportive, and at that time it was the Imperials, the male gospel group. And we were all there, we'd go up and hug him and say,

"Hey, don't worry about a thing. You feel uncomfortable, you turn around and look at us, we'll give you the finger or something. And we'll cheer you up. You just keep on singing, son. Don't worry about a thing. We're there and we ain't quitting."

"So, we reassured him. But walking to the stage, of course, they had a pull-out cart for us. All our amps and our drums were always on this cart. And it was raised up, I guess above 8 inches or something—it would be up above the stage, the actual stage you would walk on.

"So, we were all on that and they'd pull the cart out there and get us positioned in front of—well, at that time it was Bobby Morris's orchestra, before Joe Guercio. We got rid of Bobby, or Elvis did. And we're ready, but we're walking out there with him, to where he would come out.

"And you could see he was nervous. This just wasn't nervous anxiety, too, he was nervous. I think he was a little afraid, too, because he wanted to be accepted. He wanted people to like him. But he was afraid. And Charley had told him:

"There's lots of young people out there. Girls, guys. You've got fans out there. It's not like the first time. This is going to be different, buddy, you watch."

"And when the curtain went up, we started the riff, after the 2001 thing (which did not open his shows until 1971) went up and we started the A riff for, we thought, probably 'See See Rider' or something, but it was 'That's Alright Mama,' which is the same song, basically in chords. There's no difference, so we couldn't make a mistake on that. And when we got to the point in the riff and Elvis walked out, the place came unglued. The audience was standing up on tables and on their chairs and they were applauding and screaming.

"He looked, and he looked around to us like … as if to say, 'I knew it all along. They'd like me.' But he wasn't that kind of a guy. He was not an egomaniac. You could see his body lose the tension. He was ready when he grabbed that microphone and started singing—it was all over but the shouting. And the shouting didn't quit. You could barely hear him singing for the audience."

Whether one is Elvis or not, it's hard to make mistakes when one rehearses excessively. The band rehearsed even when it was no longer necessary, according to John, just to get his confidence up and let him know he had a solid band behind him that was there no matter what. In Vegas, the band rehearsed for a week or so in a ballroom that was off to the side of the showroom where the actual concert took place. It was at these rehearsals that the full band, including the Sweet Inspirations, rehearsed together. John remembers the Sweets fondly.

"We loved them," he says. "The Sweet Inspirations, three of the most beautiful, beautiful singers you ever saw in your whole life. And nice gals. Whitney's mother, Cissy Houston, was a Sweet.

Presley sets Boone straight

"Concerning my first record, 'July You're a Woman,' which was my biggest of all the five that I did—a lot of people covered that, from bluegrass groups to Pat Boone. And Pat appeared and sang it on the 'Beverly Hillbillies' TV show.

"And he sang it and then he had the record out, the cover record, and it blew me right off the charts. I was kind of upset about that because the record was gaining for me. It was doing real well, not that it would have mattered because I never got paid for it.

"Anyway, Elvis knew of my record. In fact, he used to hum it in his dressing room. I told the writer of the song, John Stewart, good friend of mine, that Elvis liked the song and I could hear him singing the song in his dressing room.

"*Darned shame Elvis didn't record that, too, John.*"

"Yeah, well, then that would have really finished me off!"

"Anyway, Elvis had heard Pat's version of it, and he asked me:

"*How do you feel about Pat Boone?*"

"Who's Pat Boone? I don't work for Pat Boone. What do you mean?"

"*Well, he covered your record, 'July You're a Woman,' didn't he?*"

"Yeah, he did."

"It wasn't anywhere near the way I did it. He even changed the words in it because he wouldn't say 'daughter of the devil.'"

"He wouldn't say the words that John Stewart wrote.

"*I'm upset with Pat for doing that to you.*"

"Don't worry about it, E. There's other songs. They'll be other records sometimes. I appreciate it, Elvis, but it's all right."

"Anyway, Pat Boone came to the show that night, that night that Elvis talked to me about that. And he sat right down in front, in the front row of the tables that came up to the stage, and he was right there center stage, looking. And Pat saw us on the stage before Elvis came out, and he looked at me and smiled, and I looked at him like, thanks a lot, Pat.

"And during Elvis's show, about half-way through, he was talking to the audience and he looked down at Pat.

"*Ladies and gentlemen, Pat Boone down here. My rhythm guitar player that I introduced you to, John Wilkinson, had a record out, 'July You're a Woman,' and (Pat put out a version that) knocked John right off the charts. And I don't think that's very nice of Pat to do that, and, Pat, I'm upset with you.*"

"Yeah! And Pat was looking like, 'Well, hey, it's just a song.' But Pat got the idea and he didn't come to any more of those shows. He didn't want to go through that again."

Elvis endured a similar indignity when Johnny Rivers beat him to the top of the charts with a cover of Chuck Berry's "Memphis, Tennessee," a song Elvis had been wanting to record for years, knowing it was a sure hit for him. Perhaps Boone's maneuver reminded him of that particular incident.

Kathy Westmoreland wasn't there. She didn't join until 1970, '70 or '71, I guess. It was Millie Kirkham doing the high voices. And Elvis knew Millie from way back. She sang on some of his early records. And Millie, beautiful woman to this day, I saw her in Memphis not long ago. What a sweetheart. She hadn't changed a bit. Got a little older, but, you know.

"So, those were the first times we had actually worked with the singers. They had been rehearsing on their own and with the records. They got the same pack of records we did. And they knew what they were supposed to do. And they opened the show, and the Imperials did a few songs. Then the comedian. Sammy Shore was the first comedian, and then it was time for Elvis.

"That idea, of course, was Col. Parker, through his knowledge of how to put on a show from the old days. You have opening acts, and opening acts, and then you bring on your star. Of course, Col. didn't realize Elvis was going to do as long a show as he did. The hotel—all hotels, doesn't matter if it's the Hilton or the Frontier or anybody—the only reason they have entertainment in the hotels at all is to attract people to come in and gamble. If you'll notice in every hotel in Vegas, in order to get to the showroom door to make your reservations, you have to walk through the gaming tables and the one-armed bandits and all that. They're not crazy in Vegas. They're not stupid. So, the hotel wants the shows to be as short as possible. That's why they don't sell tickets to the show. You make your deal with the maitre d' as to where you'll sit. You make a reservation, but there's no tickets. So the hotel wants the shows to be as short as possible. Get those people out of the showroom.

"That showroom held 2,500 people. Or 3,000—I forgot. I think it was 2,500. They want those people in, let them relax, see a show, have fun, and then get them back out in the casino. And the other thing is the only reason they have restaurants. They don't make any money on that they make it on the gambling. Keep those people happy. They want something to eat? Tell your—one of the little girls that goes around selling cocktails to the gamblers. You want a steak? Fine. We'll get you a steak. Don't you worry about it. Keep them happy. But Elvis's concept of how things should be was, 'Well, all these people have come, have driven hundreds of miles perhaps, or flown from other states or other countries, and they're going to get their money's worth. I don't care how long. I'll quit when I'm ready.'"

Elvis as bass singer?

Most fans know how much Elvis loved to sing gospel music, especially with friends and family. In fact, it was his initial ambition as a singer, to sing with a gospel quartet.

"When I want to know something about bass singing, I call Ray Walker," John says. "Nothing against JD, but Ray was with Elvis, you know, with the Jordonairres for so many years. And I ran into Ray in Nashville outside of one of the recording studios one day. And he invited me to come and have a sandwich with him, and we went over across the street, some little sandwich shop and had something to eat. And I told Ray about Elvis's appreciation of him.

"Is that right? Did he say that?"

"Sure did. He loves you, Ray."

"Because, see, Elvis always wanted to be a bass singer in a gospel group. And Gordon Stoker, the leader of the Jordonairres, told me over in Germany when we were working the same show together in Kaiserslautern in Germany, in KTown over there.

"You know, John, you know how great a singer Elvis was."

"Oh, of course, I do."

"You know the problem with that boy? He wanted to be in a gospel group and, you know, he'd sing with us. The problem with that boy is that he could never make it in a group. You know why?"

"No. Why?"

"Because he knew everybody else's part and he'd sing everybody else's part, except the part he was supposed to do!"

It seems Elvis Presley couldn't stay in one voice and would slip into the various other parts, especially the bass part!

"During some of the times after the shows when we'd go to Elvis's suite at the top of the hotel, up all night singing gospel music, Elvis would always try to do the bass part. He'd come close. He wasn't a bass singer. He was more of a baritone, if anything, or a tenor, also. He'd try. He'd get in there and nudge JD out of the way, you know, 'I'll handle this.'

"He could never get that AAaaaa (mid note to low note) all the way down. But it was fun. Elvis got the biggest kick out of trying to do that. And Ray Walker agreed.

"The kid could never make it in a gospel group because he wouldn't stay on his own part. He did everybody else's. And did it well."

— 2 —

As difficult as it is to imagine in hindsight, Elvis and the band expected these Vegas shows to be a one- or two-night phenomenon, and the crowds would drop off, and they'd have to do something else—but such was not the case.

"The showroom was packed every night and turning people away," John explains.

The opening night show unfolded beyond the expectations of everyone, Elvis especially.

"During the show, after he'd finish a song, he'd turn around and look at us like, 'They like me. They really like me. I'm alright.'

"And, you know, the Imperials and the Sweets and the orchestra would be going, 'Hey, Elvis! Hey, man! Told ya!' We'd be going, 'You got it! Thumbs up, buddy. You got it!'

"Then after the show, when the band was going, da da DA, da da DUH, the place is still going nuts, people trying to get on the stage, get under the curtain to see if they can find Elvis, and that didn't work out, because the bodyguards and the hotel security were pushing them back. We were always invited up to the top of the suite, to the top of the hotel to the Presidential Suite, up there for after-the-show, party-time kind of thing. And we were all looking forward to that because we wanted to tell him:

"See? You had nothing to worry about. You did fine, man. Look at those people out there. Did you see them? Did you hear them? Are you even aware that there was an audience out there?"

And we got up there and we were all congratulating him, and then after a while—Bobby Darin was there that night, too. He came up and Elvis was talking to him, because Darin was asking him:

"*What would you do with some of the songs I do? How would you have me perform them?*"

He was actually asking Elvis, 'What do I do?' Because Bobby's career was pretty much down in the dumper, you know? But he was back at the Sands, I think, for a one-week engagement. But Bobby was there, and Bill Medley, of course, had come up, and

Elvis loved Bill. What a sweet man. Still to this day, he is. A lot of celebrities. Cary Grant came up. What a suave, debonair guy he was. And he looked great. He had on a tuxedo, and his hair was all beautifully coiffed. What a nice fellow. "

And John did indeed get to meet all these famous people.

"*I'm a fan, Mr. Grant. I've seen you in many things.*"

"*This is a big night for me. I'm an Elvis fan.*"

"*Is that right, sir?*"

"*Oh, I have been ever since the boy first started out.*"

"*I'll be damned.*"

"*Oh, yeah. I used to stand in front of a mirror and pretend I was Elvis.*"

"*That's incredible, Mr. Grant.*"

John, knowing how much Elvis would appreciate this fan, told him all about Mr. Grant.

Elvis on Tour

"And then also there was another documentary shortly thereafter called 'Elvis On Tour,' about 1972 and released in 1973. My mom and dad had a place down on Sanibel Island in Florida, and I'd gone down for Thanksgiving, to have Thanksgiving with them down there.

"And 'On Tour' was at the drive-in in Fort Myers, which I guess is right across the way from there. And Dad saw this in the local newspaper in the movie section just as he was flipping through the paper one morning.

"*Hey, John .That documentary, that new one that you did with Elvis is at the drive-in.*"

"*On Tour, sure is. How 'bout that?*"

"*Do you want to see it?*"

"*Do you and Mom want to see it?*"

"*Yeah, we want to see it.*"

"*OK.*"

"So me and my folks went to the drive-in. And I went and got popcorn and Cokes for them and whatever. Me, sitting in the back seat watching it and mom and dad up front! They really enjoyed it, and I did, too, because I hadn't seen that one, either.

"*Johnny, you look pretty good up there.*"

"*I know!*"

"It was really fun for my folks and I to see the thing together."

"Did you know you have a very huge, very famous fan here in the room tonight?"

"Yeah, I know, Johnny. You're it."

"No, Elvis, no no no. See that man over there with the coiffed hair—looks a lot better than yours does right now—you ought to go comb your hair, Elvis."

"That's Cary Grant

"Yes, I know that. I was just speaking with Mr. Grant."

"I told him what Mr. Grant had told me.

"Are you serious, John?"

"Yep. You better go over there and straighten him out."

"So, Elvis went over and shook hands with him and they got over in a corner and started talking, I'm sure about acting. And I'm sure—well, Mr. Grant told me later, that Elvis sought his advice about getting good film projects:

"Why can't I get a really good property to work on in the movies?'"

"You're not talking to the right people. Or whoever does that for you is not talking to the right people."

"I think it was probably 3:30 or 4, something like that, we finally got to bed. And we didn't have another show to do until the next night at 8:00 for the dinner show and 10:00 for the cocktail show—well, 12:00, actually, sometimes.

"Elvis wanted everybody to be able to see a show if they wanted to. And he knew that the hotel employees that were working at the hotel, all day long, all night, people in the nighttime during the shows they would never get to see us, like the bartenders and the waitresses, this that and the other.

"So, he made a thing happen where we would do a third show on a couple of occasions, where it was just the hotel employees invited. A special show for the hotel employees. The cooks, the maids, the you name it, the people who make the hotel run. Several occasions he did that, in Vegas and also in Lake Tahoe. He'd hold a 3:00 a.m. show for the people working the graveyard shift who would never get to see him. And there was no charge. Come in, sit down, we'll do a show, even though we'd already done two shows that night—even though we're all beat and so's Elvis. You'd never know it to look at him or us.

"Fellows, we're going to do a third show. Are you ready? This is for the hotel employees."

"It wasn't like a couple, three songs, 'There you go, folks. That's me.' He did the full thing with the full orchestra, the full band, all the singers, everything."

— 3 —

In those initial shows, John got to learn about Elvis as a performer from both a working band member's perspective and from a fan's perspective. Things that one could never know until performing with him. The Elvis magic. John noticed the way he sang and performed on stage.

"He made everybody in the room feel like he was singing especially for him or her," he remembers. "Just the way he was. He wouldn't actually focus on one person. But just the way his charisma, his personality, the way he sang, the way he'd cover the whole audience. He'd turn around and look. Everybody in that show-

Elvis Presley, music fanatic

John remembers: "Elvis appreciated—you'd be surprised. I've got to tell you. Elvis was really a very complex man in his love of music. In his record collection in Graceland, he had everything from Bach and Beethoven to the Beatles to Martha and the Vandelas to Tom Jones.

"He had my records. He had Kingston Trio—he was a big Kingston Trio fan. And way back when, it seems like '58 or '59 or '60 maybe even, the Trio released an album, 'Sing Along with the Kingston Trio.' It was an album strictly with just—all the voices were taken out. And Elvis had that. And every once in a while you'd hear that thing playing up in his room and hear him singing, (singing) 'Hang Down Your Head Tom Dooley' or whatever the songs were. He was a big Trio fan, and he had a great deal of respect for just about all forms of music that he would hear.

"And, of course, his collection was massive in the gospel records. All of them, from the Blackwoods and JD Sumner and the Stamps to the Imperials to whoever else was out there. Blackwood Brothers."

room—whether it was the balcony or down front in the main showroom floor—every one of them felt like Elvis was singing directly to him. I didn't really understand that until the Vegas shows. And then, of course, the concerts when we started going on the road to the various cities across the United States.

"It had become very obvious that he had this amazing hold, like some—well, almost like Adolf Hitler could control an audience. I don't mean to associate Elvis with Hitler. What I'm trying to say is that he had that kind of hold on his audience. They were all on the edge of their seats. There was none of them sitting back. What is he going to sing next? What is he going to say? Is he going to get in a water fight with some of his buddies or his band? What's he going to do?"

The Elvis Presley performance intensity is another experience John got firsthand with every performance.

"He felt every single song. Even the ones like 'Hound Dog.' I remember when we watched 'That's the Way it Is.' Leaning down to a girl and announcing he was about to sing a lovely ballad and then belting into 'Hound Dog' and blows her hair straight back.

"He made it fun for the audience and for himself, and for us. And still sang with the same intensity. You'd see when he went into a ballad like 'My Boy' or something. He felt so intensely about that. You'd see eyes closed, and he was into it. And the audience was with him.

"You'd see when he'd get to 'because you're all I have, my boy,' you know, 'my life, my pride, my joy,' you'd see some of the people out in the audience crying. He could do that. He could make you laugh. He could make you cry.

"I have to say, Elvis is—in my long show business career, more than 40 years—he is the ultimate, the ultimate entertainer. I never saw another performer or group do what Elvis did to an audience. Or *for* an audience, either way. Even Tom Jones—he's a wonderful performer, and we're still friends with Tom, of course. Tom would be the first one to tell you—and so would Paul McCartney, but we're talking about Tom—Tom would be the very first one to say, 'You know what? If it hadn't been for Elvis, I wouldn't be anything.' And like Lennon said, 'Before Elvis, there was nothing.'

"Even though they were the Beatles. He got it right that time. Lennon didn't get too many things right, but that he got right. And that was out of respect. There were plenty of other stars around at the time, but nobody like Elvis. And Tom will tell you that until this day.

"That first run of concerts at the International lasted for two weeks. Elvis was signed for four weeks a year, in January or February, and August. The August one was the first one.

"After that, we got word from Mr. Disken, the Colonel's right-hand man—who should have actually been Elvis's manager, I

A Star Is Born

Two born stars but no "Star is Born."

When Barbra Streisand was planning to do a remake of "A Star is Born," she gave very serious consideration to Elvis Presley, even going so far as to offer him the role.

"The Colonel squashed that just (squash sound) that quick," John explains.

"My boy will be billed first. It will be Elvis Presley and Barbra Streisand or it don't get happening. And besides that, I don't like the script. And my boy—(my boy!)—ain't gonna be playin' no washed-up rock-and-roll singer."

"And Elvis stood up—that was in the dressing room—I was there."

"Look, Colonel, for the first time in my career I've got a property here that I think I could really have people respect me for my acting abilities, wherever they may be. I want to do it."

"No way! No way!"

"Why? Because of the billing?"

"That's one reason."

"Look, I don't care if Miss Streisand's at the top. Barbra Streisand and Elvis Presley. OK. Fine with me. Ladies first. Don't you remember, Col., down South? We hold doors for ladies. You never did, Col., but ..."

"He was really peeved," John remembers. "He was really pissed off about that.

"It ain't going to happen. Miss Streisand, Mr. (Jon) Peters, you can leave now."

"And Elvis looked very embarrassed because this fat chunk of flesh told them to leave. Miss Streisand at the time, of course, was one of the biggest stars in the world, too. And Elvis, while he didn't particularly care for Barbra's music, had a great deal of respect for her, as one performer would for another if they're worth their salt. And Miss Streisand, of course, was worth her salt."

think—Mr. Disken came to us to tell us of our next move.

"*We're going to go on the road right after the Vegas gig. We're going to go down and we're going to play the Houston Astrodome.*"

"The Houston Astrodome? There's 50,000 people in that place. So that was the next big step for Elvis, because he had never played for an audience that big, ever. Elvis came to us, too, after this announcement.

"*Did you guys hear we're going to do six shows there?*"

"Yes, sir, we sure did. Mr. Disken came and told us."

"*Oh, good. Man, I don't know about doing that. It's a ball field basically. It's enclosed. I don't even know if the place is still standing. I don't know. How are we going to get our sound out from being at the pitcher's mound to all 50,000 people? What are we going to do?*"

"*Well, that's up to the sound guys.*"

"So, Claire Brothers out of Pennsylvania were our sound people and they took a look at the Astrodome and they figured out how to do the sound. There were no baffles in the place, so there were no acoustics, basically. But we got there.

"And again, there was a revolving stage that they brought out, and it was right over the pitcher's mound, dead center in the middle of the Astrodome. And the singers were on there, and us. There was no room for an orchestra, so we had to do with just the rhythm section. And then Elvis, they put him in a Jeep and had him stand up, and they drove all the way around the Astrodome twice. And he was waving at the people and of course the place was coming unglued. Fifty-thousand people standing up, and hollering and screaming.

"He didn't want to do an outdoor stadium and the reason was he was afraid the sound wouldn't be right. People paid a lot of money, came a long way to see him. And if the sound was crappy then he would feel very, very badly about it. All he was concerned about was his fans—the fans, and the best job he could do for them, sound-wise and otherwise.

"So, we got to Houston and they had us over for a sound check, of course. But not Elvis. Felton from the control booth, wherever it was in the place, asked me to sing,

"John, would you get up there and sing a song, let the guys play behind you, so we can kind of get an idea of what Elvis's voice is going to sound like through this?"

"OK."

"So, James started off on 'Mystery Train.' I did 'Mystery Train,' and at the end of it—ended just like Elvis would do it if he was going to do it, and Felton came on the mics over the sound system.

"Nice job, John! You ain't Elvis but you're good."

"Thank you, Felton. I appreciate that."

"I think we got it. I think we're OK."

"I loved Felton. He was a great guy. Anyway, we couldn't use our own amps because they just weren't—even if we mic'ed them—they wouldn't be powerful enough to get the sound out with Elvis's voice to 50,000 people. So, what they did was rent us Beatle amps—those big tall amps that the Beatles played. Henceforth, evermore known as Beatle (Vox) amps. So we all had those.

"James didn't like them because he was used to his Fender Twin. That's all he ever played. And I didn't like it because I wasn't used to it. I had a Fender Super Reverb that I was using, the four 10s. Nice amp. And I couldn't figure out this Vox, but we got it figured. It was hard to work because we weren't used to it. The Beatles could plug into it just fine because that's what they used. But when you change instruments or change equipment, it really presents a problem—or it can.

"The first show we did there, they brought Elvis out on this Jeep, like I said, and rode him around the perimeter, the side there, of the arena, and let him off behind the stairs. He got up on stage and he shook his head like, 'I dunno.' We started off doing the same show, 'That's Alright Mama,' or 'CC Rider,' at that time I think he was starting to do. We couldn't really hear. The monitors on stage that were aimed at us so we could allegedly hear what was going on didn't work very well.

"So, we were going on, watching him, his moves—he could hear us fine and we could hear him occasionally. But we would just go ahead and play like we normally would, knowing that he'll hear us and know where to come in. And the show went great. The place came unglued.

"After the fourth show—Charlie Pride was booked into playing the Astrodome also. Charlie plays acoustic and his band is very low key, not like we were, but we all loved Charlie Pride and we were all friends with him. And Charlie came over to the motel where we were staying, and he came hunting for me and James, and he found us, and we brought him in and were talking to Charlie—what a sweetheart he is.

"*Fellows, I don't know, man. I heard the show today. I was over there. I don't know how you guys did it. I'm scared to death to do this place.*"

"*Don't think we weren't. You'll be fine, Charlie. Everybody loves you. That beautiful voice of yours, you'll be fine.*"

"*I don't know, guys.*"

"*No, you'll be fine, Charlie.*"

"*Can I get you guys to play for me?*"

"*You ought to speak to Elvis about that, Charles. We don't know. I doubt it.*"

"Because we were already going to go somewhere else, down to Arizona or someplace. Tempe, at the university. But those shows were Elvis's first exposure to that many people in one place to sing to. And he worked really hard. He would turn around so people behind could look over us and see Elvis. He really had concern for people who couldn't see from the front. But then again, the stage turned 180 degrees and then back, so everybody could see pretty much, unless you're up where the rats and spiders are, in the top rows, which is kind of difficult, I suppose.

"He did wonderful shows there. The only trouble really was, in a place like that were there's no baffles or anything, no real acoustics, is that after you're finished playing the song, it's still coming back at you from the echo in the place. It's kind of confusing. But we're supposed to be professionals, and we were. We overcame that. He'd say, 'Next song. Let's go.' And we'd start playing, even though the last song was still coming back to us, we'd go ahead and play. And the audience loved it. They loved him."

After those initial gigs in Las Vegas and at the Astrodome, Elvis began to loosen up and have more fun on stage, with the audience and his bandmates. Pranks became common, whether a double glass of water on Glenn D. Hardin or some girl's hurled panties that he'd take and put on JD Sumners' head, anything to just loosen him up.

"He meant no disrespect to anybody at any time," John explains. "It was all just to loosen him. Have a little relaxation for a moment there, and then he could go on and sing. And that started in the first gigs in Vegas. He'd change the words in a song to make them funny, things like that."

Filmed in July and August of 1970, over the course of six concerts, a concert film was shot to be titled, "That's the Way It Is," mostly filmed at the International. This was the band's second trip to Vegas. Despite the presence of the film crew, Elvis reassured the band to continue to TCB.

"Don't pay any attention to them. They're going to be wandering all over the stage, so don't worry. Let them go where they need to go, and don't hit any of them. If they get close to me, don't worry about it. It's all right. Have fun. Just keep playing like you have been, guys."

Elvis even felt the need to reassure the audience.

"I guess y'all know we're making a movie here tonight. Don't let the cameras throw ya. And please don't throw the cameras, if you can possibly avoid it, you know?"

This was the first documentary of his resurgence into the limelight of being a performer and Elvis wanted it to go right, which it did, according to John.

"The first release of 'That's the Way it Is' was incredible. And now there's been the re-release of it (on DVD) that has more footage, and actually more shots that covered more of the people on stage than just Elvis."

Surprisingly, it wasn't the first time John watched himself on a screen. While living in Los Angeles, he'd done some TV shows with bit parts on "Baretta" and (William Conrad's show) "Cannon," but this was in a different capacity than as a musician backing up Elvis Presley.

"When I first saw that—actually, when it first came out, we

were in Florida. And we had a day off down there. Sometimes we'd go in to where we were supposed to be and we'd have a day for just anything we wanted to do—go shopping or go to the movies or whatever. And I remember Sylvia Shemwell, of the Sweet Inspirations, suggested we see it.

"Hey, guys? 'That's the Way it Is' is showing at the movie theater downtown. We're going to go see it. You wanna come?"

"Sure, let's go down and see ourselves on screen."

"So, we hired a couple of cabs, I think, we stole one of the limousines from the hotel, I don't know, and we drove down there and went in and saw it for the first time. And we laughed at some of Elvis's antics, and we'd see ourselves, and the girls would say, 'Aren't I so pretty there?' And then, of course, we'd play with them, too.

"See, Sylvia, we're pretty there, too!"

"And seeing ourselves in the capacity that we were, working as a unit behind this major star that we know as Elvis Presley, was really pretty exciting. There weren't many people in the theater. But those who were there kept looking around, 'Who the hell are they?' They didn't know who was there. But it was quite an exciting time."

*"We do two shows a night for five weeks.
A lot of times, we'll go upstairs and sing until daylight ...
gospel songs. We grew up with it.
It more or less puts your mind at ease.
It does mine."*

— Elvis Presley

"A live concert to me is exciting because of all the electricity that is generated in the crowd and on stage. It's my favorite part of the business: live concerts."

— Elvis Presley

CHAPTER 10

My friend, Elvis

— 1 —

RIGHT AFTER THE ASTRODOME, Elvis and the band did a short tour. All of the band's tours were usually of short duration, a couple of weeks at a time, perhaps 30 days. Once after a tour, Elvis invited John to visit Graceland to hang out for a couple of days before returning home. He agreed.

"I didn't have any real responsibilities. I said I'll call the person who's watching my cat and watching my house, and check and see what's going on. Yeah, I can do that.

"That was the first of our many one-on-one conversations. When Elvis got home, his guys that worked around him all had families, and he had told them:

"*Go ahead. Go home with your families. I'll be alright.*"

"His housekeepers and his cooks were all there. But on the night we got in, he was ragged tired, so we didn't do anything. He went to bed, and I went downstairs and racked up on the pool table, if I recall. And then the next morning or early afternoon, Elvis got up and came down. And it was a Sunday and there was football on— Sunday afternoon football—so we were watching that and just talking like two buddies would.

"*Look at that stupid quarterback. He didn't have to throw that damned thing. I could do better than that!*"

"*I bet you could, E.*"

"Then we got talking about music, our lives, our private lives.

'Are you happy? What's going on? Is there anything I can do to make your life better?' Like you would your best friend. Just chit-chat stuff. Those private times with him were my most precious memories because he could open up. He opened up to me about a lot of things in his life.

"Look at this, Elvis. Let's face it. You were a truck driver working for Crown Electric in Memphis. You were making, what, 20 bucks a week or something? I don't know what it was. And then all of a sudden, it seemed to everybody—although it took a matter of time—all of a sudden, you're the biggest star in the world. You're a phenomenon. Nobody had ever seen anything like you, and hasn't since. All of a sudden, you're a musical sensation. How did you feel, coming from where you were born and coming from the kind of poverty you were in, and your daddy moved you and your Mom up to Memphis, and you got a job in a paint company first, and then you drove a truck for Crown Electric. You were a truck driver. And then the magic thing happened. You met Sam Phillips and you made a recording for your mother for Mother's Day or her birthday or something. Just a gift. So you stood in front of a microphone and you heard yourself back for the first time. And from there, everything just skyrocketed. How did you feel?"

"Man, it was a hell of a ride. I really didn't know what was happening. I didn't understand. I was scared. I just made that record for my mama. It was nothing special to me. I didn't think it would catch anybody's attention, except my mama. That was it."

"But he talked about this meteoric rise to where he was.

"Just the most incredible ride. I never expected anything like that. After the first initial successes, I realized I wanted to be a singer, and I felt like I could do it on my own if I had somebody who could play behind me. Because as you know, Johnny, I'm no guitar player."

"Yeah. I'm very well aware of that."

"But he talked at length about that.

"By that time, I had quite a lot of fans who liked the music I was doing and liked to watch me perform. And I have a great love for them because they're the ones filling up the seats. Because you well know, John, it's no fun playing to an empty house."

"I know that."

"I realized then that people, these fans, were very special and I owed them a lot. I owe them my career and my life, actually, because otherwise I probably would have stayed a truck driver."

"And he talked about that guy at the Grand Ole Opry, who said, 'If I were you, I'd go back to driving a truck.' He said that hurt him so deeply. That scene in that movie with Kurt Russell ("Elvis") where he busted his guitar open on the wall and all that—he did that.

"I was just so frustrated. I thought this (Grand Ole Opry) might be a break. Because my mom and dad listened to the Grand Ole Opry, and I was going to be on the Grand Ole Opry, and that was going to be such a thrill to my folks. And then they just basically jerked the rug right from under me. And they were right. I wasn't cut out for the Opry, but still I felt like I had a place there and it would have been a wonderful chance for me, but I got booted."

"And he talked about that, about how hurt. And he's a very sensitive guy. He had deep emotions, and he could get hurt very easily.

"There's a lot of things that hurt me—people complaining about my music, saying that I was lewd and crude. I had no intention doing anything like that to anybody. John, you know that."

"I know that. I know that. But they didn't back then. There were a lot of preachers and PTA people and parents and what have you that came down on you pretty hard."

"Yeah, they did. And it hurt my feelings really bad. Because all I wanted to do was sing and have people have a good time. I meant no disrespect or harm to anybody."

"I know that. And people know that now. But I know there were several instances you played down south in some of the larger auditoriums in an open arena a couple of times down in Florida where the police actually took films of you to determine by their codes or the city codes whether you were breaking the moral rules or something."

"Yeah, yeah, they did. And I never got an indictment against me but they felt because of the pressure on them, they had to film it. I sure wish I had those films back from them to see what was so bad that I was doing. You look at some of the people on stage now, John. Some of these guys, they're doing worse than I ever did."

"Yeah, you're right. You're right."

"So, we had long conversations about his career from the time he got his first little guitar to the time with Sam Phillips and on, and he indicated he was really happy with the way things had gone. And I asked him about Col. Parker.

"*I don't want to talk about that.*"

"OK, fine."

"You see, John, I shook hands with him when I was 19 years old, or 18 years old, and I said, 'OK, Colonel, you handle the business and I'll do the music.' And we had an agreement that way. I shook hands with him. And you know very well my handshake's good."

"Oh, I know."

"It was good then, and it's good now."

"I know."

"I don't personally like the Colonel. He doesn't treat people right. Mr. Disken could do the same thing the Colonel's doing. He knows the same people and he treats people a lot better."

"Yeah, we all feel like that, too."

"So, he didn't want to say too much about the Colonel, but he talked more about us, about the relationship he felt with not only just me but with the other people who worked with him on stage. Elvis was one who would never say, 'These guys work for me.' He would say, 'These guys work with me. This is OUR show rather than MY show.' He always included everyone else in it.

"So, those one-on-one times were very special to me. I recall that we were at Graceland one time and we rehearsed because he was going to try to record there. And the recordings did not come out the way he wanted to hear it, and he told everybody to go home—except me.

"*Johnny, you stay back for a minute.*"

"OK."

"Let's go get a pizza and some Cokes and play some pool."

"Elvis, does that mean you want to leave Graceland and go out and do that? You can't do it. There's too many people out there, *and they'll follow you, and there's not very much I'll be able to do to help you get out of there in one piece. You can't do it, man."*

"All the other guys are going down there and doing that."

"Yeah. But they're not you. I'll tell you what I'll do, though. I'll order pizza. I'll order pizza in, and I know where your stash of Coca-Colas are. I'll go get that and let's go down and play on your pool table. I'll stay here and play on your pool table for awhile."

"Well, OK."

"Can I use your phone?"

"Yeah."

"So, I called up and got two or three pizzas ordered in. And I took them down to the pool room, right off to the jungle room there downstairs, or the TV room, rather, and we sat down there and ate pizzas and drank Cokes and played pool for a couple, three hours. And then some of his guys came back and asked Elvis about

JLL

There is no love lost for Jerry Lee Lewis from John. In fact, during the interviews for this book, he referred to him only as "JLL." John shared a story that contributes one reason for his lack of affection for JLL when Mr. Lewis saw fit to visit Graceland one evening, circa 1976:

"He was, as usual, drunk or drugged or something. And he came screaming up to the gates of Graceland in his car, and he got out of his car and he was waving a pistol around.

"I'm the one who's supposed to be living here, not you!"

"And I believe it was Uncle Vester who was tending the gates.

"If you were supposed to be here, you would be."

"But, you know, he wasn't meant to be. He raised so much noise down at the gate, I guess, Red came down and told him to shut up. And JLL had a pistol and was waving that around the air.

"So, Red fired a shot at him because he feared for his life. Jerry Lee is crazy. And I think it nicked his shoulder, and he went away. JLL was very jealous, extremely jealous, of Elvis's success. And there was a time in JLL's life when he actually did sell more records than Elvis, and you would think, or at least it would be for me, I'd think, 'Hey, that's pretty darned good. Maybe team up with the guy, or let's work together on some things.' But that wasn't to be. Jerry Lee believed that Jerry Lee is Jerry Lee, you know? The high and mighty Jerry Lee. So that was not to be."

the pizza."

"Where'd you get the pizza?"

"John went and got it for me, ordered it up."

"What are you guys doing?"

"Well, we're playing pool, as you can see, and eating and having a good time."

"Well, hell, we would have taken you out."

John answered for Elvis this time.

"Fellas, you don't understand. I know there's a whole bunch of you big guys and you could probably take care of him alright, but he wanted me to take him out, and I told him, 'No. Can't do it.'"

"Well, John, we're glad you were here. Thanks, John, for taking care of him."

"It's your job to take care of him, actually. But some of you just didn't seem fit to do it, did you? You wanted to get out of here and pick up your girls for the night, or do what you wanted to do."

"So, we had long conversations about the people who worked for him and against him (laughs) and about all the members of his group on stage, and really got some insight on how he thought. We talked about where he wanted his music to go. Which direction? Or the same direction?

"What do you want to do? What do you have in mind?"

"I want to do some big things, like 'American Trilogy,' 'My Way,' 'My Boy,' things with a big orchestra."

"He wanted to do some dramatic music so he could show that his voice was more than 'Heartbreak Hotel' and 'All Shook Up.' Some real intense music.

"I'd love to do that Paul Anka thing, you know, 'My Way.' Sinatra did it and had it out."

"Well then why don't you do it?"

"Well, I don't know how to go about getting the rights to the song."

"Elvis had lots of problems getting song rights—because of Col. Parker.

"There's people you have here that know how to do that. You want me to mention it to Esposito tomorrow?"

"*Well, yeah.*"
"*OK, fine. I'll take care of it. Don't worry about it.*"
So I told Joe the next day.
"*Elvis wants to do 'My Way,' the Paul Anka song. He wants you to get the rights to the song to be able to record it and to perform it.*"
"*OK, I'll do that. He told you about that? What were you doing here?*"
"*At his invitation, I stayed, after the botched recording session.*"
"Joe felt kind of bad about that, I guess, because he wasn't invited, and none of the other guys were."

— 2 —

John, like the rest of the band, soon discovered martial arts through Elvis. Elvis started his martial arts when he was in the Army and found it to be not only fun but something that could continually challenge him.

"That's what Elvis needed throughout his life, a challenge, a real goal to reach, and get his teeth into and hang on like an old bulldog," John explains. "Martial arts was that way for Elvis. And he took to it quickly because he was very agile, and he had a very quick, sharp mind. So martial arts came to him very easily, when his instructors would show him things to do. He preferred the Kempo version of karate, the Korean version.

"Master Kang Ree was the one who gave him his 10th degree, I believe. Ed Parker, of course, big old giant, just as sweet and gentle as he could be, but he could snap you like a twig, of course.

"And I took lessons from Ed, and Chuck Norris, also. And I originally started, as far as I'm concerned, my thing with Karate I took basically self-defense, because Elvis and his guys, they loved to roughhouse. So you had to be able to throw some punches back, whether you connected or not.

"Elvis loved martial arts. That was something he could excel in, second only to his ability as an entertainer. He was really good.

And there was a time when he wanted to do a Karate movie. Not like the Karate movies you see on cable today. Not that there's anything wrong with them; they're fun. But he meant to have a movie that was really instructional, that showed the finer points, and to impress on the point that Karate was not just to destroy. That it was about discipline and concentration, to broaden your mind. I thought it should be that way, too."

Like 'A Star is Born,' Elvis's martial arts movie was not to be. The busy touring schedule simply did not allow the time to put the film together the way he wanted to.

"I think there was some filming at some time, maybe just to get an idea for him, to have something to base on. But I don't know if that has ever surfaced or not. I kind of think it hasn't but I don't know for sure.

"I'll clear something else for you, too. It was said toward the end of his life that he was very depressed, that there was nothing left, and all that. That's not true. Elvis had all kinds of plans for what he was going to do later on. He had tour plans. He had movie plans. And not just movie plans with him as an actor, but for him behind the camera, as a director. He wanted to get into that aspect of the film.

"And he would have done really well at that. But again there wasn't enough time. His health wouldn't let him. His body was just wearing out."

It's been documented in Presley biographies that Elvis believed he was on earth to entertain and bring people happiness. Elvis also devoured books on various religions, philosophies and spiritual thoughts. John remembers well this deeper side of Elvis.

"He was fascinated by all different kinds of religions and how they might go from a divergence to one common line. I think most of them do at some point, but there are differences in all the major religions.

"He told me that he really believed he was on this earth to make people happy. To lift them up out of despair, if you will. That was one of the reasons he loved to give away expensive gifts, like Cadillacs or Lincolns, or high-end Pontiacs or diamond rings or things like that. Not just because he was showing off his wealth. Because he really felt like he was doing something good for somebody."

Even as John and Elvis grew closer as friends, John refused to take advantage of that friendship in any way, even if it disappointed Elvis. Elvis didn't only buy cars for strangers on occasion; he once offered one to John.

"In 1970, I had just bought a 1970 Opel GT, a little sports car, and it had the flip-up headlights and it had the gear shift on the floor. And you pulled that up and your headlights flipped up and went on. It was really a great little car. I just loved it. Every man at some point in his life has got to have a sports car. And at some point, every man should have a luxury car, for no matter how long. But every man—perhaps women, too, I don't know, but every man, I know—should have that. And that was my little dream sports car.

"And we were over at the MGM lot doing the 'That's the Way it Is' rehearsals, that they filmed what everybody's seen on the DVDs or actually TV. I drove that up and parked it right there and got out, and we did the rehearsal and had a break in the rehearsal and Elvis saw the car.

"That's a sharp little car, John. You like that?"

"I sure do."

"That's good. Those are cute."

"Nothing more was said about it. So, I go home and the next day I come in for rehearsal and I parked in the parking lot, and I walked in. We did the rehearsal and at the end of the rehearsal, Elvis approached me.

"John, you see that Cadillac out there? Well, that's yours."

"Elvis, I already have a new car. I bought me a new car a few days ago. You saw it the other day."

"Well, that's your car."

"No, no, Elvis. I can't take it, man. I can't take your car. I already have a car, and just I don't want your car."

"He got a really strange expression on his face."

"Nobody turns down a gift from me."

"Well, I sure can. Let me tell you this, Elvis. You might be able to buy friendships of other people around you perhaps. But you can't BUY my friendship. You can pay for my talent, whatever that may be, to play guitar for you and sing for you, whatever, but you can't buy my friendship. You can earn it, like I feel like I've earned yours. You know, we're friends. But you can't give me a Cadillac and feel like you've bought me, because you haven't."

"And I know that wasn't his intent. He just wanted to give a car away, because he'd given cars to a lot of the other people. I guess it was my turn, as far as he saw it.

"*Elvis, I'd just as soon you gave it to somebody else. It's not that I don't appreciate it, but I don't need it and I really don't want it. And if I hurt your feelings, I'm sorry, but I'm not going to take your car. I've got my little Opel GT sitting out there in the parking lot and that's all I need. I'm a happy man. I'm working with you, which was a childhood dream. My dreams have come true, Elvis. I don't need your Cadillac to make it solidified, concrete in stone.*"

"I think I actually saw tears in his eyes because nobody, I mean nobody ... so many people around him always had their hands out: 'Elvis, I need a new car, my ashtray's full,' kind of thing. And Elvis had the hardest time saying no to anybody. He really did. And he would give people whatever they wanted. That's why many of them stayed on so long, because they knew they could say, 'Elvis, you know what? There's a leak in the roof of my apartment. I need a house.' And he'd buy them a house. Or, 'I'm out of money in my checking account, Elvis. I need $5,000 to get that straightened out so I can pay my bills.' And he'd take care of it.

"But they always had their hands out. I didn't have my hand out. And I wasn't going to take his car. It was a beautiful Cadillac. But I'd actually hurt his feelings. The next day when I came in for rehearsal, he wouldn't even talk to me. He'd look at me, but he wouldn't talk to me. The following day after rehearsal, he (finally talked to me).

"*John, come here a minute. I can't believe you turned down a car from me.*"

"Well, I told you why. I think my motives are right."

"*Nobody ever has turned down a gift from me. They'd take that car right away.*"

"Yeah, but, Elvis, you know what? You've given me this TCB necklace—a beautiful necklace, this one here—you've given me a *beautiful onyx stone ring in a gold setting. You've given me gifts. But you've given me gifts when you were giving everybody else a gift, too, and I don't want to be singled out this way."*

"Thanks, John, for being the way you are. I just never expected anyone to turn down a car from me. You're the only one who did. Put that in your history book."

"Then things were alright. He felt better, I think, knowing that there was at least one person around that was associated with him who wasn't looking for handouts."

The Generosity of Elvis

"Down in Memphis," John explains, "Elvis and some of the guys were driving downtown. There's a Cadillac dealership down there. And they were looking out the window, and there was this old black lady looking in the window at this shiny Cadillac, and obviously she didn't have money to buy a Cadillac, much less a Plymouth or anything else. Elvis told whoever was driving,

"Stop the car for a minute."

They got out, Elvis walked over to this lady and stood beside her.

"Ain't that pretty? That's a really pretty car, isn't it Ma'am?"

"Sure is."

"Hang on a minute right here, Ma'am, will you? My fellows will look after you for a second."

He goes in, talks to the salesman.

"See that lady there? That's her car? So draw up the papers. I'll sign, we'll take care of the money or whatever."

He comes back outside.

"Ma'am you still like that car? You still think it's the prettiest thing you ever saw?"

"Yes, sir. It surely is."

"Well, that's your car. Go on in and claim it. Go on inside. The gentleman standing right there beside that window right there, he knows all about it. You just go right ahead."

"What?! Who are you?"

"And she looked again and then, I guess recognized him, Elvis Presley, for God's sakes. And he got the biggest kick out of that. Not making fun of the old lady. But here was a lady who probably had a few more productive years in her as far as holding a job or doing whatever, taking care of her home, whatever, she probably had family, a husband and several kids, most likely.

"And he did something wonderful for this poor person who would never have a chance at having something that nice. So, he got the biggest kick out of making people happy, whether it was with his music or his legendary generosity. And those stories of his generosity were not overblown. They really weren't."

The TCB band's guitar section: James Burton and John Wilkinson.

CHAPTER 11

The Touring Years

— 1 —

As the 1970s progressed, the TCB Band continued to enjoy ecstatic audiences and excellent performances. Many adventures confronted the band that are well documented. One well-known incident involved a rumored assassination attempt against Elvis. John recalls that incident very well.

"There were death threats quite often and why, who knows? Except a jealous guy who wants to make notoriety by saying, 'I killed Elvis Presley.'

"Anyway, Elvis's security team took it real seriously, as did the hotel. And they called the FBI, and of course the state police and the local Las Vegas Metro, and they lined that place with security officers, in the showroom, and they felt like, when Elvis was doing 'You've Lost That Loving Feeling,' he'd turn his back to the audience and the spotlight was right on his back and he felt like that would be the perfect opportunity for someone to shoot him.

"And he instructed his bodyguards, if that happened, to get the assassin, and rip his eyes out and his tongue too. So, that he couldn't say, 'How about me? I'm the one that put a bullet in Presley.'

"It was a frightening thing. Should Elvis go on stage that night when a threat was supposed to be carried out or should he not?

"*I'm going on stage. I'm not going to let some punk scare me off stage.*"

"*Elvis, you don't have to prove nothing. You're fine. Everyone loves you. You're alright. You don't have to go on tonight—even the hotel said you don't have to go on. Give the law enforcement agencies time to, a chance to process this information to see if they can get to the bottom of this assassination threat came from."*

"No, *we're going on stage."*

"So, he's doing 'You've Lost that Loving Feeling,' and he was sweating. Who knew if there was some guy with a folding rifle in the balcony or floor, with a pistol, who knew? And of course there were no metal detectors at the entrance to the showroom, at that time, that would set it off if someone had a weapon on him. But we started the song, he sang it, he was looking around, but he sang it and it came off great, the song sounded great and he looked good doing it. And nothing happened.

"Still, the police and the other law enforcement entities stayed for the entire week after the night that it was supposed to happen just in case because maybe whoever was going to do it got spooked by seeing so much security. But nothing further happened. But it was scary. Elvis's daddy was especially worried, as were all of us. We didn't want to see our boss hit the ground, red stain on his back.

John recalls Elvis's reaction to the whole idea:

"I don't understand why anyone would want to hurt me? I'm just singing, trying to make people happy. You know, that's what I do. I can't do anything else. Why do they want to hurt me?"

"And it really bothered him. I don't think it was so much that there was a chance that he could get killed as why someone would want to kill him.

"What have I done to them? What I have done to this person that makes him so upset that he would want to kill me? I really don't believe I have ever, ever, intentionally hurt somebody. Or made anybody's life bad."

"It was really puzzling to him. And it continued to bug him throughout the rest of his life."

However, as John previously explained, there was also plenty of silliness going on to keep the mood fun. Usually, it was the TCB Band who had to bear the brunt of Elvis's humor. However, one night the band got its revenge.

"This was maybe the third engagement in Las Vegas, I think. If you look at the 'That's the Way it Is' film, when he starts to do 'Hound Dog' he gets down and he tells the audience that this is a tender love ballad, and he gets down on his knees and right in their face, (singing) 'You ain't …' and he'd do this almost every night, do that routine.

"And with all the practical jokes that he pulled, all of us figured, 'Hey. We got to do something. We can't sit here like idiots and take all this abuse,' in good fun of course.

"One of the stage hands, I forget his name, he was a wonderful guy, had an old bassett hound an ugly old bassett hound but he was so sweet, and he brought that dog to work every night. And I don't know who came up with the idea, I really think, forgive me Ronnie Tutt, I really think this was you, went and talked to that stagehand.

"What they decided to do: This dog, this old bassett hound loved a certain kind of treat the man would give him. And the dog would chase this treat. What was going to happen was when Elvis got down on his knees and (singing) "You ain't …" we were going to roll that treat out and hopefully that treat would land right under Elvis's nose and that dog would be right in his face.

"Well, OK, come the next song we signaled the stagehand though we didn't have to because he knew the show. Elvis got down and we're looking over at the stagehand and he goes, 'right.' And we're going, 'Throw it, throw it,' so the stagehand rolls that treat out there and the dog goes after the treat, and as luck would have it, that treat rolls right under Elvis's face, and he looked, 'What the hell is that?' and here comes this dog and he saw the dog before the dog got to lick him but the dog did give him a kiss. It was great.

"*Oh man, which one of you guys came up with this?*"

"We got him. He didn't expect anyone to retaliate but he was so known for his practical jokes that we had to do something. Once again Ronnie, I'm sorry if I busted your cover son, but … it had to be done."

Undoubtedly, the prank was a playful reminder to Elvis of his appearance on the Steve Allen Show, where he had to wear a tuxedo and sing "Hound Dog" to a basset hound in a top hat!

"But he laughed and the audience thought it was the funniest thing they had ever seen. That night, Don Rickles was in the audience. And of course, with Rickles in the audience you know you're going to get it. Don will nail you. He was sitting in the audience and he was so tore up with laughter he couldn't say nothing, thankfully. 'Cause Elvis knew Don and whatever Don would say would be taken in good spirits but Rickles was just falling out. So, we're all really proud of ourselves, patting each other on the back, saying, 'We got him. That'll teach you.'

John played victim to Elvis's pranks onstage as well.

"This was also in Las Vegas and all day long, I don't know what day it was, might've been a Friday or Tuesday, who knows, but all day long Elvis and the guys had been up in the suite that he had for his people and somebody decided that we were going to play cowboys and Indians.

"And so somebody went out and got water guns, water pistols. And they were chasing each other around and shooting each other with water pistols and all this. Come later in the afternoon, Elvis had to get some dinner in him and get ready for the show. Everything was fine. They had a good time that afternoon, they're playing, everyone's in good spirits, and now it's time to go on stage. We're on our cart, they pull the cart out, we're in front of the orchestra, we're all set up, we're ready to go with our vamp, the key of A for 'That's Alright, Mama/See See Rider' and Elvis is standing in the wings, ready to come out at a certain point that he knew.

"He came out and I could see him, he had something in his right hand, but I didn't know what it was. It looked pink to me but I couldn't tell what it was. Maybe it was a scarf or handkerchief. And, as he walked out, past JD Sumner and the Stamps, and the Sweet Inspirations and he stopped, turned around and took this water pistol, and he shot me, right square in the center of my guitar.

"Now, it doesn't take a rocket scientist to know what happens to metal and electricity and water. And I was wearing metal fingerpicks and I was playing, and that water hit and you could see a blue arc go up my fingerpick and the strings, and it knocked back a couple feet—I didn't fall down, but it knocked me back because it was a shock. He stood there looked, giggling inside, that silent laugh, you know, hee hee.

"Elvis, why did you do that."

"Because I have a water pistol and you don't; na na na na naa na."

"And he continued walking across the stage, acknowledging the applause, acqueicing the audience. So, that thing with the dog was especially sweet for me!"

Later, however, Elvis approached John to make sure he wasn't hurt from the shock.

"John, are you OK?"

"Yeah, why?"

"I'm sorry, man, I'm sorry. I was just having a little fun. I'd forgotten that water and electricity ... I'm sorry. You're not hurt too bad are you?"

"Nah, I'm fine. I know you're just having fun."

"But he realized it could've been serious. But like I said, there was no way he would intentionally hurt one of us. Or embarrass any of us, intentionally. But have fun, yeah. What do you think we signed on for?"

During this period, Elvis acquired a love of firearms and law-enforcement badges. Elvis loved being deputized by whatever law enforcement agency protected the city he happened to be playing and he carried his collection of badges with him on tour. John remembers these times very well.

"He had a fascination with firearms. He had collection that included everything from 12-gauge shotguns to Derringer pistols. Like some people collect porcelain owls, he collected guns. He was very pro law enforcement. And he really appreciated the hard work of the local police, state police, in all the cities we played, to try to make things easy for him to get in and out of the venue and hotel and taken care of. He really appreciated that.

"And he would ask some police officer or state trooper, 'Is there any way I could get a souvenir badge? I collect badges.' And they would say, 'Sure Elvis.' Nine times out of 10 they would take their own badges off and say, 'Here you go Elvis, you can have that.' And they'd get another right away, and tell their boss, 'Hey, I'm not wearing a badge, I gave it to Elvis.' And yeah, he collected those things, because again, it was a hobby.

"I used to collect guitars. I couldn't play them all at once, and you couldn't wear all them badges all at once, but he collected uniforms and badges and guns. He was very proud of his gun collection. He had some marvelous pieces. Really nice."

— 2 —

John's "signature song" with Elvis became "Early Morning Rain," written by Gordon Lightfoot. Eventually, Elvis performed it in his set and John remembers how this happened.

"Now, there's two stories about that," he says, "but the one I tell is what happened, as far as I'm concerned. This was at RCA Studio C, where we were rehearsing. And we'd been going at it for three or four hours and Elvis finally said, 'I gotta take a break guys. I gotta hit the men's room' or something.

"He walked out of the studio. So we knew he'd be gone 10, 15 minutes, something like that. So, I was sitting in the corner of the studio, just doodling around or something, and I was playing 'Early Morning Rain' softly. He comes walking back in and walked over to me.

"What are you playing, John?"

"Well, it's a song called 'Early Morning Rain.'"

"Well, I know 'Early Morning Rain'—who wrote that?"

"A friend of mine named Gordon Lightfoot."

"Oh, I know who Gordon Lightfoot is. I have some of his albums at home."

"I know you would love singing it. And he's a wonderful singer/songwriter, Gordon Lightfoot is."

"I betcha I could do that song."

"So, I was playing it while we were talking about it and he started singing it, and I was harmonizes it with him.

"Geez, that's a wonderful song, I just need to do that. Hey you guys in the control room, could we get that down?"

"We're already rolling."

"It was on tape, and then he really enjoyed that. I was playing that since the early '60s anyway, it's one of my favorite songs. And again, he like the way I fingerpicked so when he started introducing people on stage in Las Vegas by their name, he wanted us to show off a little bit, so James work his magic, as only James Burton can, play something fantastic.

"They had recorded 'Early Morning Rain' for the Elvis album, 'Now,' in 1972. And it's not my … it's James doing it that's not the way I started the thing, I finger-picked it differently. But it worked out nice and it sounded good.

"Anyways, when Elvis started introducing people on the stage, he passed by me. Why exactly I don't know, just had a lot of things on his mind. And he'd say,

"*On lead guitar, from Shrieveport, Louisiana, James Burton. Play something James.*"

And James would just mesmerize everybody, like he can, and Ronnie would play something on his drums, and Jerry would do some fantastic things on the bass.

"*Glen D. on the piano.*"

"After the second time he passed me by, when the show was over and people were putting the guitars in their cases, putting them away in a locked music room the hotel was kind enough to give us, Red West came down and he was doing something on stage. He saw me in the music room.

"*John, Elvis asked me to tell you he was sorry he didn't introduce you. He meant nothing personal by it.*"

"It's OK Red, I understand. He's got a lot of things happening in his head. It's alright. He wouldn't hired me if he didn't like me."

"That's right. That's right, John."

"And the next night—now I didn't expect to be introduced

because I hadn't been, it's been enough to be on stage with him, I didn't care—but the next night he comes by, he's introduced Kathy Westmoreland, now I'm next, if he's going to introduce me. And he walks in, and he's just before me ...

"On rhythm guitar, from Springfield, Missouri, John Wilkinson. John play me something."

"Play what? I don't know what to play."

"Well, son, you better play me something or you'll be working for Wayne Newton tomorrow night."

"I didn't want that! OK, and all I could think of to do really was 'Early Morning Rain,' so I started picking it the way I had done it when he first heard it in RCA, in Los Angeles. And he started singing the song and the verses and the chorus, and I could tell he was ready to end it and don don donn don and I ended it.

"Thank you John."

"And the audience applauded. And he went to James, Glenn D., Ronnie—that became my signature song because when he introduces me in all the shows, that's what I'd play but that became—I don't remember where it was, someplace on the East Coast—he was introducing us and I played the thing in the key of C, in the D finger capoed up two, you know what I mean? And that was fine with him, at that time. So, he introduces me.

"John Wilkinson, play it John."

"And he started singing it a little bit, and he stopped.

"Wait, wait, wait a minute. I'm not J.D. Sumner, John. Can we raise that up a little bit? Have mercy on me John, I just woke up. Don't make me sing it down there that low."

"So, I was always trying to be one jump ahead of him. I had a capo in my hand back there and put that on there real quick; we were in C, I'll make it D, and started playing it.

"Hope this is good for you boss."

"Yeah, that's good, that's what we'll start doing from now on."

"You got it—no problem."

"So, that's how 'Early Morning Rain' came about.

Another trademark of Elvis shows in the 1970s was the introduction music, Richard Strauss's "Thus Spoke Zarathustra," made famous in Stanley Kubrick's classic, "2001: A Space Odyssey." John remembers distinctly how the music came to be part of the prologue to an Elvis concert.

"He had seen the movie and heard the theme, Strauss," John recalls. "Priscilla told him that would be a wonderful thing to open and have you come out on stage; that would be really powerful. And he agreed, 'Yeah that would be fun.'

"So, we started doing '2001' and then Joe Guercio came to Elvis and us with some bad news.

"*You can't do '2001' anymore: Something about copyrights, or I don't know.*"

"You would think that that was public domain at that time with Strauss long gone.

"*Joe, you compose something, that would be as powerful, if possible.*"

"So, when you look at 'On Tour' and some of the footage from the concerts, you'll hear something that sounds sorta like '2001,' but it's not, but it does have the horns, and the dom-dom dom-dom, the kettle drums but that's something Joe Guercio composed to take the place of the '2001' theme. And it sounded fine. And it was in the same key, so we weren't left hanging.

"And then eventually somehow it was worked out with RCA perhaps, or Guercio, and his group, and the copyright situation. It got resolved to where we could use '2001' again. But for awhile there I guess they said, 'Nope, you can't use it. It's copyright, you got to pay us everytime you use it.' But he didn't feel like it was that necessary. If it was one of us that had written it, and if it was me for instance, and I'd gone to Guercio and say, 'You know, this piece I wrote is getting an awful lot of exposure. I think I'm due some extra money, Joe.' I'm sure Elvis would've said, 'That's right. Whatever it is Joe, just go ahead and pay him.' But I probably wouldn't have done it anyway, and fortunately I didn't have to do it because it wasn't my orchestra piece. But again, Elvis was very fair and he could have said, 'Joe tell the copyright people we'll pay it.' But Joe composed this piece that was marvelous and we all liked it, and Elvis liked it too because it did have those highs where it would send chills up your back. And you could see Elvis shaking. And then when he'd come out on stage, he was more than ready. Good 'ol Guercio."

The 1970s rewarded Elvis fans with some great new music. Elvis indulged himself as never before in this period, trying many different songs and musical styles but with an ambition to pepper his shows with some very dramatic numbers. "An American Trilogy" is a perfect example of this type of number. John remembers when Elvis and the band worked it into their set.

"Well, 'American Trilogy' was put together and written by Mickey Newbury, wonderful folk singer, country artist, guitar player, and a nice fellow too, by the way. Well, he didn't actually write it. He took three folks songs from Americana and put them together in medley, which basically it was.

"'Battle Hymn of the Republic'/'All My Sorrows' and he put all that together and played it himself. And he got quite a lot of play of it down south, especially in the Nashville and Memphis areas. Elvis heard it on the radio and decided he'd like to do it his way—cause he felt like it, well, Mickey has a wonderful voice but he's not a power singer, like Elvis can be.

"But Elvis felt something in that song that Mickey had put together. And at that time, he really wanted to start doing something that was big orchestra, big emotional music to show how mature his voice really was. And 'American Trilogy,' he picked that. And he brought it up to us in rehearsal one time.

"*Have you guys ever heard Mickey Newbury's 'American Trilogy?'*"

"And we all had. I think all of us were fans of Mickey, too. And I had it on an album at home.

"*Maybe you guys can listen to that and work out an arrangement for me, and let's try it out tomorrow night. I know the words and if you guys could work that out.*"

"So, we all got to RCA a little earlier than we usually would and Glen D. had written out charts primarily for the orchestra but also asked us if we had questions how it goes. If you took it right from the record, you know where all the changes come, the minor chords and all that.

"So, we played it through two or three times with Glen directing us, making sure.

"I think we got it. Let's see what Elvis thinks when he comes in."

"Elvis comes in and we run through just for him to warm up and relax some of the old things, just for him to get ready.

"OK fellas, let's try something new."

"And hopefully, Lamar or somebody would have some new demos to listen to for new music for his albums. And Glen reminded Elvis of 'Trilogy.'

"Elvis, you talked about 'American Trilogy' the other night, I believe we got it down, we've been working on it here. You wanna hear it? You wanna try it?"

The King and the Greatest

In 1971, those who cared were very much divided about the first heavyweight championship bout between former champion Muhammad Ali and current champion, Smokin' Joe Frazier.

Ali was banned from boxing and stripped of his title years prior for refusing the draft on conscientious objector status, famously saying, "No Vietcong ever called me 'nigger.'"

The more "patriotic" types were for Frazier, feeling Frazier represented patriotism while Ali, draft dodger and Muslim (not to mention "outspoken") represented the Enemy. Elvis, patriotic though he was, did not choose sides in this conflict.

"Well, Elvis had no prejudices," John explains. "He didn't see color. All he knew was that he liked them all: George Foremen, Frazier, Ali—all of them. But Ali had come to see the show two or three times and had come backstage, and he's a gentleman. He wasn't the braggart that you see on TV, 'I'm the greatest.' I mean he was probably the greatest. He would stop by the dressing rooms and shake hands with us. You don't realize how big Ali is, and how big that hand is, until you see that big meat hook coming your way to shake your hand.

"And he went down to see Elvis and they talked for quite awhile and Elvis would mention Ali in some of our private conversations.

"What did you think of Muhammad Ali, John?"

"I think he's a great guy and a hell of a fighter. I don't think there's anybody out there that can take him."

"Of course, we were proven to be wrong a little bit later but he didn't say anything about the comparison of Ali or the reason why whites would go for Frazier over Ali or the draft thing or whatever. He didn't mention that at all. Not to me anyway."

"Sure, let's do that."

"So, James started that (hymns the melody) and then Elvis started (singing) 'Oh, I wish I was ...' and it worked out so well, it was just that one take, that he said we got to record this and put it in the stage show.

"We gotta do it. We gotta lock it in."

"We worked on that for, even though he had it down perfectly, he was never (finished) until he felt like he had it. Well, we felt like he had it, but what are you gonna tell him, 'No, boss, you don't gotta do it anymore?'

"We did it some and he felt real comfortable with it. At home, Charlie Hodge told us that he worked on it and had recorded it. They put it on tape for him in the studio when we ran through it that one time and gave him the tape. He took it home and worked on his moves and how he wanted it presented on stage to his audience. When he came in the next time, we were rehearsing or recording something.

"Let's do 'America Trilogy.' I just wanna see how it feels without me not facing you but doing it as if we were performing it on stage."

"We had it and he had it—of course, he had it before but this time he really had it. It was right. Elvis was such a patriot. He loved the United States and he had such respect for our armed forces, all the men and women who are in the armed forces, fighting for freedom and to try and make freedom available to other people in the world. Just as he felt when he went into the army himself, his whole thing was 'I'm helping them,' and that fit right in with his heart, and the way he would give."

Songs like "Trilogy" and "You Gave Me a Mountain" gave Elvis the chance to really utilize the power of his vocal abilities. Some suggest that more songs of heartache and loss, such as these, found their way into the set because Elvis himself became more depressed. John denies this.

"Those songs gave him an opportunity to be more dramatic and show the real power that he had in his voice."

— 3 —

About July or August of 1972, now that Elvis Presley proved to be a sensational stage draw wherever he toured, Colonel Parker booked the band to play Madison Square Garden for the first time. Like Las Vegas, New York was a town Elvis had not played since his early days of touring and like Las Vegas, he was nervous because of it.

"Oh yeah, four shows, Madison Square Garden," John states. "The Colonel had originally just booked one show. But the demands for tickets were such that they had to schedule three more shows.

"Elvis had not played New York since the early days when he was on tour. He was a bit reluctant because he had heard the rumors, the reputations of New Yorkers being cold and loud, and very unappreciative of performers, and gave performers a hard time and blew them off the stage and things like that.

"He knew he had a lot of fans in the East Coast and the Northeast. From that aspect he wanted to do it but he was really reluctant 'cause he felt like he—he had the feeling like he did the first time in Las Vegas.

"*Are they going to laugh at me—what are they going to do to me?*"

"But again, all of us tried to reassure him.

"*We're here. Take it easy. You'll knock 'em out in Madison Square Garden. It'll be a complete cold, technical knockout or just a full, flat-out knockout. Don't worry about it.*"

"We rehearsed real hard for that. Our suspicions proved true. He tore 'em up. The album shows it. (By the way that's one of the few times when he introduced me to the audience he actually said, "Wil-kin-son," not "Wil-ker-son.") But New York audiences were actually very cruel to Jackie Kahane, the comedian. They basically booed him off the stage. And it was so bad, that Al Dvorn, who was the announcer for the show, and who coined the thing, 'Elvis has left the building,' actually had to make an announcement to the audience.

"*Elvis has asked me to ask you to please have respect for his friends that are going to come out before he does to entertain you. Please show them the same respect that you would show to him. Jackie Kahane, the fine comedian, the Sweet Inspirations, JD Sumner and the Stamps Quartet, all fine people, so please honor their talents and treat them as you would Elvis.*"

"And they straightened up after the first two shows. Still, you'd hear out in the audience one of these jackasses, 'We want Elvis now!' I can kinda understand that, because that's what they bought the tickets for. But the tickets that they bought they were getting more than their money's worth. 'Cause the Sweets and JD Sumner and the Stamps and Jackie were wonderful action of themselves, terrific performances.

"And they straightened up a little bit. But that (reaction) brought Elvis down and after the shows, when Jackie encountered such negative response from the New York audience, Elvis hugged him.

"*Don't worry about it. We'll get out of here pretty soon. We'll go someplace where we're really wanted.*"

"But he enjoyed the New York shows and they recorded that, and shortly after that we played Chicago and we played the Chicago Stadium, which has now been bulldozed and the new facility is across the street, I think. But the sound in the old Chicago Stadium was better than the sound in Madison Square Garden. And I think they should have recorded that but for history's sake and posterity they recorded it in Madison Square Garden, because Elvis had never done that.

"In fact, not very many people had done Madison Square Garden successfully. There had been other acts there but not really as successful as Elvis was, or that they knew Elvis would be. 'Cause RCA at that time was headquartered in New York. And of course, they plastered the city with all kinds of posters, radio ads, TV to promote Elvis. And the response was unbelievable. The album was a rush mix and released only a week or 10 days later but it was a big seller."

Call him Duke

John met many famous people because of his friendship with Elvis, including the biggest stars of the time, such as Cary Grant and John Wayne, known to everyone as "Duke" (not "the" Duke). Duke's real name was Marion Morrison and when he'd walk to school every day with his dog, Duke, the locals would call out, "Hey, Duke!" He hated his first name so much he eventually adopted the dog's name and became Duke instead of Marion. The name "John Wayne" is purely a Hollywood invention like "Joan Crawford" or "Kirk Douglas."

John recalls meeting Duke and getting the specific name instructions.

"We all loved John Wayne. As all of us were respectful of people with stature like that, and Elvis, 'cause we called him 'Mr. Wayne,' and he got downright hostile about that.

"You want to address me you call me Duke."

"OK, Duke."

"But he had said, 'You call me Duke.' He did that to Rick Nelson too, in 'Rio Bravo.' Rick was a really respectful young man, too. Rick told us:

"If you all get around John Wayne, call him Duke, because he about had my head when I didn't."

"But Rick was a nice fellow. He would naturally call you, 'Mr. Moretti.' First time out, we'd say, 'Rick, come on. We can call you Rick cause the whole world calls you Rick or Ricky (later years it was Rick) but he was as gentlemanly as Elvis and a wonderful fellow. I miss him, too."

"I've never gotten over what they call stage fright. I go through it every show. I'm pretty concerned, I'm pretty much thinking about the show. I never get completely comfortable with it and I don't let the people around me get comfortable with it, in that I remind them that it's a new crowd out there. It's a new audience and they haven't seen us before. So it's got to be like the first time we go on."

— Elvis Presley

"I believe the key to happiness is: someone to love, something to do and something to look forward to."

— Elvis Presley

CHAPTER 12

Aloha, people of earth!

— 1 —

WITH MADISON SQUARE GARDEN and the Astrodome behind them, Col. Parker decided to go for the ultimate: a live worldwide satellite broadcast of an Elvis concert that would raise money for charity. Best of all, the performance would be in Hawaii, to John's and every one else's pleasure.

"Oh my God," John remembers. "Eight solid days in Hawaii and only two performances. Yeah, that was a terrible deal. God that was hard for us. I'm sure glad I didn't have to do that again!

"We had heard rumors floating around that there was something big for Elvis that we were all going to be involved in but we didn't know what it was. See, Charlie Hodge had shared a dressing room with me at the Hilton and he came from Elvis's dressing room one night all smiles and giggles.

"What's the matter with you Charles?"

"You'll never guess what we're going to be doing, Johnny."

"What?"

"You can't tell nobody now."

"OK, go on, what?"

"Well, we're going to Hawaii."

"That's nice. What are we going to be doing in Hawaii?"

"Well, I know what I'm going to be doing in Hawaii. What are you going to be doing in Hawaii?"

"He said we were going to be doing a satellite special with Elvis.

"You didn't hear it from me."

"And later on, Mr. Diskin, the Colonel's right-hand man, came in and sure enough:

"*Are you available from this date to this date? We have something going that we think will be a real, real test of Elvis's drawing power. Are you available between January this date and January this date?*"

"*Yes sir, I'm available.*"

"*OK. Well, we'll be in touch.*"

"*Fine, thank you Mr. Diskin.*"

"Later, another day had passed and he comes down again.

"*How would you like doing a TV special broadcast all over the world on a satellite from Hawaii?*"

"*What do you mean what would I think? I think it would be terrific. Nobody's ever done that before.*"

"*We're drawing up the contracts now. When you get home, I'll mail you what you need to sign your releases and use of your likeness and name that has to be done because of the unions.*"

"*Fine. I'll keep those dates open and no problem.*"

"So, he went to all the other guys and they said 'sure' they'd love to do it. And the girls, the Sweets, said sure, you betcha, and JD Sumner—he's a big boy—'You betcha we'll do it.' You could hear him rumble all the way down the hall in the basement of the Hilton.

"We were all excited about that. Elvis held rehearsals for that. And again, we were at RCA at the Studio C to rehearse and he was all excited about it. But understandably he was somewhat nervous, because this was the biggest event, ever, that they had planned for him, besides Madison Square Garden. 'Aloha' was going to be the biggie. And I remember thinking at the time, 'I wonder if this is his swan song? After this magnificent satellite thing that we're going to do, and I'm sure it's going to be magnificent, I wonder if he's retiring or something.'

"I maybe he felt like he wanted to go out with a bang and this certainly would've been that. But when he talked to us in the studio when we were rehearsing:

"And there'll be more to come guys. You just hang on to your teeth and britches, the train's moving."

"That dispelled that feeling inside me. We knew right then that he was looking forward to the show.

"You know, I don't know how it's going to be. I've been on TV before and I've done movies. Live satellite, broadcast to 43 countries or something. Can't make any mistakes fellas, or they'll know."

"What was planned was to do, well, we did some rehearsals there in Los Angeles. There was going to be a big dress rehearsal (performance). We were going to do the show as Elvis had planned it, and that was to be, ostensibly for the technicians, the satellite guys to get all their ducks in a row, make sure their equipment was in sync with the satellite and all the hookups and everything it takes to do that. To make sure all that and the recording situation was airtight, that everything would work smoothly from the minute that the lights went down to the time Elvis walked on to the time Elvis walked off, because that was a very expensive proposition to do that. I don't know how much that cost, I don't have the figures at hand.

"But you know it had to be a monumental figure to put on something like that. So we did the dress rehearsal and the whole place was filled. There was 2,000 people from Japan that came and got to that show, which we now know as the 'Alternate Aloha' on DVD and video. And that went real well, as smooth as clockwork.

"But prior to that show, the director, Marty Pasetta, had come on the stage and we were lined up, ready to start, and went up to Elvis.

"*Elvis, here's what we're going to do. I'm going to have your band over here, your singers over there, your orchestra will be split here, and here and I'm going to have two winding staircases coming down and I'm going to have two dancing girls come down there ...*"

"And we thought, 'That's not an Elvis show. That'll be really tough for us not to all be together,' and Elvis very gently said, and we were standing right there:

"Um, Mr. Producer, that's not how it's going to be. This is how it's going to be: My band guys are going to be right here behind me; my singers are going to be right over here to my left; my orchestra is going to be together, not split; and there will be no dancing girls and winding staircases. Or, if that's not suitable for you, we're going to go home. There will not be a show. I will pack up everything and my guys and ladies, and off we go back to the mainland."

"And Mr. Pasetta just turned to him, ghostly white.

"Well, OK Elvis, we'll do it that way."

"Thank you, sir."

"And he turned around to us.

"Fellas, nothing's going to be different. We're going to be doing the show the way we have been, the way people like it."

"That dress rehearsal turned into a fundraiser for the Kui Lee Cancer Foundation, and raised $75,000 that night. He misspoke when he announced it onstage when he said it was $25,000. And then come to find out later that he matched what the show brought in and gave his own check for $75,000 to the Kui Lee Cancer Foundation. Which is like him. I wouldn't have expected anything less.

"Then the night of the big show, the next night, Elvis was pacing in his room, up in the Rainbow Tower, just to the right of the Hilton Hawaiian Village Hotel. He was nervous. Because this was it. There ain't no second takes on this one, this one is the big enchilada. So, when he came over to HIC, the building where it was taking place, he looked great. I never seen him look so good. His weight was great, he was tan, his hair looked great, and he had that wonderful mischievous thing in his eyes, and grin.

"We're going to get 'em tonight guys. Thirty four to nothing."

"And in fact, we did. And again we reassured him.

"Man, this is one of the biggest moments in your life, at least that we know of, this is going to be the ONE. Don't worry about a thing. Everyone is going to give you 150,000 percent. What you want you'll get and more. Hopefully, just everyone (the sound and lighting people) else has it right."

"That's right. We got it, now it's up to them."

"So, he was excited about it. And as you could see in the alternate show, and if you see the 'Aloha from Hawaii' broadcast (version), you'll notice very little difference. Some people say the alternate show has more energy perhaps. I don't feel that way. I feel both shows were the way Elvis should perform when he was really on his feet.

"And he looked wonderful and some of the reviews of the show to this day still piss me off. There was a reviewer in San Francisco who said, 'Elvis looked awful. His voice isn't there anymore. He should retire. He's not Elvis anymore.'

"Well, he looked fantastic. He has a special suit that was built especially for that night, the American Eagle suit. I never seen him look better. The only time I would've seen him look any better was in 1969, when he was going back to live performing. He had worked real hard before going back to Hawaii to look excellent and he did. He looked fabulous.

"And everyone else who saw him on stage would say the same thing. This reviewer said he slurred his words—he did not slur his words. Everything he said, he sang, you could hear crystal clear. And it was no mistakes, hesitation on his part, he just knocked 'em dead. It was perfect. A perfect show.

"And you gotta give credit to the technicians too. 'Cause they spent long hard hours, even after we were outta the building, we're going to the bars to have something to eat, and they're back there still working with the satellite and the lights and the sound making sure the baffles were turned just exactly right and they monitored those real well. I gotta give a lot of credit to those guys and girls who were there."

John recalled a humorous incident one morning in Hawaii over a drink with JD Sumner.

"After that first night (the 'alternate Aloha')," he says, "I went back to my hotel room after I had gone out for a little while, and I had woke up a little early for some reason. I should've slept until noon, but I didn't. I was up at like 7:30 in the morning. We hadn't gotten in until about 3:00 am. But for some reason I couldn't sleep and I got up and I grabbed a shower and got dressed in my Hawaiian shirt and shorts and flip-flops on my feet.

"Went downstairs and went out the side of the Hilton Hawaiian

Village Hotel there and walked outside there and there's a—not too far away—there's a grass roof shack, a bar on the beach. I looked at that and thought, 'I've had breakfast already, it's OK. It's time to have a chi-chi or something.'

"So, I was walking that way and I saw someone sitting at the bar. It wasn't just somebody, it was a big somebody.

"I wonder who that is at this time in the morning?"

"Well, it was JD Sumner. So I walk up to the bar there.

"Hey J, how ya doing buddy?"

"Fine, John," in that big 'ol bass voice of his.

"What are you doing here?"

"I'm having a drink. Can't you see that?"

"Yeah, I can. I was just going to do the same thing. Can I buy you a drink, J?"

"Naw, I'll buy you one though. What do you want?"

"I want a Mai Tai."

"So do I. Bartender, make that two."

J bought me a drink.

"Let's take a walk for a minute."

"We walked out on the beach, got down by the water's edge over there when the ocean comes up, and if you turn left you can see Diamond Head, beautiful sight when the sun comes up, gorgeous. And we were talking about the show and how well it went.

"JD, last night did you know there were 2,000 Japanese to come over here to see Elvis on the Love-You Mission? And how else could you describe it, it was a wonderful audience."

And JD took me by the shoulder and turned me around.

"Listen to me boy. Don't you ever forget that on December 7, 1941, 2,000 of the Japanese came down on the Diamond Head over there on a Fuck-You Mission!"

"That's what he said!

"That was then. Remember, it's government that goes to war, not people. And let's try not to forget that in that war on both sides, some very brave men and women lost their lives, not just us, the U.S. The Japanese, the Germans, the Italians, everyone who's involved in that war lost some very brave soldiers and men and women serving in their own armed forces.

"And JD knew that, but that's just what he said because he was real quick. And we continued to walk and we were drinking our drink and he said:

"*We don't want to get too far away from that bar, John, our drinks are getting low.*"

"You have to remember JD was drinking like two quarts of Early Time bourbon a day, straight out of the bottle. I don't know how the hell he did it. He claims it gave him his bass voice. He was a wonderful singer when he was young.

"*OK, JD, let's turn back then.*"

"*Are you going swimming?*"

"*No, not at this moment, I'm walking with you. If you want to go swimming I'll go with you.*"

"*Naw, naw, I don't want to get my hair wet. It takes me a long time to get it right.*"

"We went back to the bar and had another drink.

"*I gotta meet with my guys, the singers, I'll see you later.*"

"Off he goes. Whether he met with the guys or not, I don't know. I thought that was funny, early in the morning, the sun just barely up, and there he was. I loved JD. He was like a second daddy to us. He really was. He was that kinda guy—and Elvis loved him. They knew each other from way back. When J would let him in the back door of the venue where the gospel singers would be and let Elvis watch the singers and sing with them a bit. Well JD Sumner, what a wonderful human being. Couldn't help but love him, he was a terrific man. Miss him, too."

— 2 —

Even Elvis Presley worked to maintain his voice.

"For those who don't know about performing in a hotel in the desert, there is a condition known as 'Vegas throat,' because Vegas is dead in the middle of the desert, and it's very dry, and most performers are constantly drinking water to keep their throats and vocal cords moist.

"And Elvis was consuming massive amounts of water 'cause he could feel a tickle in his throat that, sure as the world, signals he's either getting a cold or the flu, or the dryness of the climate is affecting his throat. And he sang hard and that's why he drank so much Gatorade and water onstage to keep his throat moist."

Now it is told: Elvis Presley relied on Gatorade and water to keep his throat healthy. He used to joke about it, calling its consumption "aiding his gator," and looking at the bottle as if it were "used" Gatorade.

"He consumed massive amounts of both. He was in Vegas, and the dinner show he performed beautifully and the show went just fine but we noticed that his voice was not what we were used to. It was kinda strained. We noticed he was swallowing a lot and he was having a difficultly.

"Then the cocktail show, the midnight show, was usually the show that he would do in the hotels and would be on the par of a about an hour or hour, 15 minutes, which the hotels hated, of course. But he cut that short. It was about a 40-minute show, or maybe 45 minute. At one point he skipped a bunch of songs in the lineup, the alleged lineup that we could never really trust, and he turned to Glenn D.:

"Let's take it home."

"This meant 'Can't Help Falling in Love With You,' from the movie 'Blue Hawaii,' and he always closed the shows with that. We thought, 'What the hell?' So we did it, and he took his bows and walked offstage and we didn't hear a word, went to our dressing rooms and got changed out of our show clothes and suits, and got ready with our regular street clothes.

"And later on that night, or early morning, we got a phone call from Mr. Diskin again, our liaison between the Colonel and us, like Esposito was the liaison between Elvis and us. Mr. Diskin called each and every one of us.

"*Elvis is having to cancel the engagement. His throat, he just can't do it. He's going to have to cancel it. He's got Vegas throat and he's going to get sick, so that'll mean we have to postpone oth-*

er things."

"So, we were all packed up. We were paid for the whole thing.

"You all got contracted for this time, you set aside this time when you could've been doing other things, and you will be paid for the whole. The Colonel asked me to make sure I told you that."

"OK, Mr. Diskin. Who's coming in to do the rest of the show? Who's taking his place?"

"Bill Cosby."

"Oh, great. OK."

"I met Bill on a couple occasions. So, before we left, I stayed another night, so we could go see Bill. And Mr. Cosby was a wonderful fella. He made sure, we got word to his people, his (version of) Joe Espisito, his Mr. Diskin, that we wanted to come see the show. Since we weren't going to be on stage we wanted to see Bill.

"So, Mr. Cosby and his people arranged for us to have front row and second row seats so we could see Bill work. Now there is a class act. Bill is just … and what a nice fellow. Not just a terrific entertainer but he's just as sweet, down home as you want to meet. There was that one time when Elvis had to cancel out, and then he had to cancel out again for the same reason: because he was violently ill and to this day I know it was because of the impacted colon problem. But again, we got a call from Mr. Diskin.

"Elvis is going to have to cancel, he's sick. There's no way he can continue this gig."

"Who are you bringing in?"

"Peggy Lee."

"Really?"

"So, we all did the same thing. One of us, or Mr. Diskin, called Peggy's Lee's representative and asked, 'Can you make reservations for our guys and girls to see Ms. Lee?'

"Word came back, we could see the cocktail show. So, all of us did whatever we did during the day and marched into the showroom and again, had the front first two rows and Peggy Lee. What can I say about Peggy Lee? She's a legend in herself. She did a real good job. It wasn't Elvis but she drew her crowd, a much older crowd, and they responded very well to Ms. Lee.

"But that's the only two times I can think that he had to cancel a show in Las Vegas. But it was a combination of that second time of that impacted colon and that Vegas throat. It wasn't a case of overdose or anything like that, as some reporters saw fit to print, 'Well, he's on the drugs again. Had to leave Las Vegas. He's washed up.' Pissed me off. I remember calling a couple of those reporters myself.

"*You don't live with him. You don't know what he's like. You have no idea what you're saying. What's the deal? You didn't get a free seat at the concert so now you're writing bad things about him? 'Cause he had to cancel the concert he must've been really spaced out, huh? You're wrong.*"

"It really made me mad to take on my boss like that when he's not around to defend himself. So, we all felt the same way and we wrote letters to the newspaper and the other reviewers around the nation who claimed they knew what happened. And we all wrote letters and signed them and said, 'You guys are full of shit. You're wrong.' So, we tried to defend our boss the best way that we could."

One famous incident during a show involved several fools who decided to rush the stage, unprepared for a very prepared Elvis Presley.

"It was just an incident, it was too bad. Fans applauded, they thought it was part of the show! But it was a serious attempt. 'Cause these guys had been overheard waiting in line to get in the showroom and see how far they could stretch Presley. They'd heard how big and bad he was, but they didn't know how big and bad Sonny and Red, and Dick Grob, and Big Tex, who was one of the hotel security officers there, assigned to our group and Elvis. They tried to get on stage; one of 'em made it and Elvis kicked him real good, it was all karate stuff, knocked him back on the table. And a bunch of glasses and stuff went flying and all that. Red, Sonny, Dick and Tex got the rest of 'em, and they were readily escorted out of the showroom. They were not allowed to stay.

"But Elvis apologized onstage.

"I'm really sorry about that, ladies and gentlemen. I have no idea what prompted that. Somebody wanting to hurt me, I guess. And I don't understand that."

"And he was perplexed onstage.

"The stage is sacred ground. You don't get on stage unless you are a performer. And they weren't. They weren't my guys. I have no idea why they did that, ladies and gentlemen, I'm sorry. I hope nobody got hurt over there. Did anybody get hurt over at that table? Red, anybody get hurt?"

"Yeah, Elvis, everybody's alright."

"When these idiots got up, drinks spilled on people, but nobody complained. In fact, they applauded Elvis."

— 3 —

As the early '70s became the mid-70s, Elvis began to noticeably gain some weight. Although the media negatively exaggerated Elvis's appearance, he was having some weight issues.

"I think it was very exaggerated although he did not look as slim and trim as he did for the Madison Square Garden shows or the 'Aloha' show or his reemergence into the performing scene in '69," John explains. "But that was water retention so he was a little 'puffy'. But it didn't affect his performance at all."

Another aspect of Elvis's shows were increasingly lengthy monologues in which he would talk to the audience about anything from karate to his life. Again, much negative interpretation is given to this but John offers the reality of these monologues.

"There was a time in Vegas or Tahoe when he came out and instead of wearing his usual jumpsuits, he had on his karate gi. And he went into a long monologue, a philosophy, and we were taken by surprise.

"What are you doing Elvis? Let's sing? Play some music. That's what these people are here for."

"And Red and Sonny were taken by surprise, too, as was the Colonel. He went off on this rambling monologue about religion, and karate, and a cohesive thing about the two of them. And the audience was shocked as well, and some people got up and left. 'Cause that wasn't what they had come to see. And the press reported that they thought he was wired on drugs. Why would he go off rambling like this? It had to be some kind of outside influence. 'Cause Elvis sings, he don't do monologues, that kind of thing.

"So, the press did get on that about him. They were close to being right except he wasn't wired. He was just charged with ... he felt like he wanted to share his inner feelings about his mystical experience with the audience, thinking they would enjoy it. They didn't."

John agreed it probably made the audience uncomfortable.

"Yeah, they thought they were seeing an Elvis that was over the edge. Something was definitely wrong. He's crazy, something's going to happen. Is he going to overdose? And at that point, we really began to believe he was doing illegal drugs, which he wasn't. But he could have been influenced by those prescription drugs that night. As sometimes that will happen with anybody. You act different, perhaps. But he wasn't wired."

At another point in 1973, Elvis finally fired Colonel Parker during a heated argument between the two. John remembers the incident and offers his insight about the relationship between Elvis and Colonel Parker.

"It just goes back to what kind of person the Colonel was and Elvis was really very hot about the fact that Colonel nixed the deal with Ms. Streisand and 'A Star is Born,' and he felt like Colonel was not really acting in his best interest. Because that was really out of character for Elvis, because we told him:

"Get rid of him. Let Mr. Diskin take over."

"I shook his hand when I was 18 years old and I don't go back on my handshake, and you guys know that. I can't do it."

"They did have a big blowup and Elvis threatened to get rid of him and get somebody else from William Morris agency or Mr. Diskin or somebody. But I think he felt like, well he had gotten word from the hotel on how much the Colonel was gambling. And where'd that money come from? Well, the money came from Elvis being out working.

"Well, the Colonel was actually taking more than the normal amount of percentage a manager or booking agent can take, usually between 10 and 15 percent—never higher than 20. And Colonel was taking 50 percent and sometimes 75 percent. And Elvis got word of that and he was pretty upset about it. So he was yelling at the Colonel.

"You're not taking care of me, you're not looking after my best interests. What are you doing? The only reason you have me out on the road and doing concerts and stuff is so that you can gamble it away!"

"And Elvis wasn't a gambler. That wasn't one of his vices. He did want to play 21 one time but he couldn't just go down to the casino with his bodyguards, it would've caused a whole disruption in the casino and that wouldn't have sat well with the hotel. Elvis did want to try and play 21. So the hotel made arrangements for a dealer and table to be brought up to the suite so he could just play. And he played $5, $10, or $1 a bet.

"So, he wasn't a gambler. There was another reason for it too: He came from abject poverty, where there was no money, to a situation to where he had millions. So, when he was growing up there was no extra money ever to throw away on candy or soda pop, so he had a real appreciation for money. His daddy, Vernon, was in charge of the money around Graceland, and Vernon got real upset with Elvis too.

"Son, you can't be giving away all these cars and things, it's costing money."

"Which translated to money that Vernon wasn't putting away in his pocket. Vernon was making plenty, just living off of his son. But he wasn't a gambler.

"As far as the Colonel: He didn't like the fact that his, this Colonel Parker, that this legendary manager, was out in the casino in front of everybody to see, just throwing money away. And he was playing the roulette wheel, which everyone knows is the worst bet in any casino. And he's betting racks of black ($10k each rack), which was thousands of dollars a spin. So, it kinda got to Elvis from the standpoint of,

"What am I working for? I'm trying to work for my fans but actually I'm only working just so you have money to gamble with."

But as far as threatening to fire him, I think he did say something like:

"I can do this without you."

And Col. Probably said:

"You think so? How'd you get to where you are without me?"

In October of 1973, Elvis went into the hospital for breathing problems. John feels it was just another time when exhaustion took over. He was touring too much. But it was in 1974 that the band really noticed the beginning of a physical deterioration.

"In '74, we really noticed it. We opened up a tour in College Park, Md. And when Elvis came up the stairs under the stage, he walked right by me and we noticed he just didn't look well at all, like jaundice or something. He was terribly bloated. And Kathy (Westmoreland) had been with him for awhile. I remember looking at Kathy.

"What happened? What's the matter?"

And she shook her head, and mouthed back to me.

"I don't know."

"But he could barely walk and he was really sick. He could barely walk onstage, stumbled over the microphone stand a bit. He was very unsteady on his feet and he forgot the words to songs, which up until that time he hadn't. We shouldn't have done that tour. He should've been in recuperation, gotten some sort of help. But true to form, he got on that stage, even when he was in such pain that he couldn't move, he'd always get on that stage 'cause he felt he owed it to his friends.

"But it was a obvious to us from 1974 on that something terrible was wrong with Elvis and his health. He was having difficulty walking. We could tell that his stomach was upset sometimes because he'd have to leave the stage.

"On that famous show, what was it, Baltimore? The famous fall-down-on-the-stage thing on his back. Well that, the newspaper reporters really butchered that because he'd done that several times at shows, lay on his back and would still be singing, crossing his legs, just to tease the ladies.

"But we could see that something was definitely wrong, healthwise, with him. He didn't look the way that we had seen him before. He suddenly, well, people would say that he was fat. Obviously, his suits weren't fitting him like they had. He was squeezing into them the best he could. When actually, it was water retention, it really was.

"But, he had so many, people don't understand, he had so many things wrong with him physically, glaucoma for one—a horrible twisted colon that meant sometimes it was impossible for him to go to the bathroom for five or six days. That'll hurt for anyone, I don't care who you are. And later on, it was announced that he had bone cancer, that had spread out throughout his whole body.

"So, he was on a lot of pain medication, but it was all prescription medication. There was never any illegal drugs; I never saw him take anything. But Kathy Westmoreland said that he was having trouble sleeping so he would take prescription sleep medication so he could sleep and get some rest. And because those things had a real effect on him, he had to take some things to wake up.

"But that started over in the army. Things to stay awake when on guard duty, which is not what you're supposed to do but that's where, that's how that got started. But it's no secret to anybody that he abused prescription medication. He did. His doctors also wouldn't say no to him, 'cause he was handing out Stutz Blackhawks.

"If you do this for me, I'll give you one of them."

"Wherever he went with him was a PDR: a physicians desk reference. And he probably knew more about prescriptions than doctors did, or at least that's what he thought. And he'd go in there and see what medications wouldn't interact with this other prescription he was taking and he'd tell the doctors what he thought he needed. He was his own worst enemy.

"So he got these doctors, especially that Elias Gonham, down in Las Vegas, the fight doctor, he'd give Elvis anything he wanted; write out prescriptions. He'd take them and he'd get hooked on 'em. And at that time I remember there was no Betty Ford Clinic, for someone who has an addiction, whether it be medications or alcohol or drugs or whatever, to go and get cleaned up for six months or a year or whatever.

"So, he was caught between a rock and hard place there. He had to have these medications; Sonny was right when he, or Red said:

"*Elvis, you gotta quit doing this. It's killing you.*"

"*Man, I gotta have 'em, I gotta.*"

"And it was a cry for help but there was no real way to help him. 'Cause the doctors wouldn't say:

"*No, Elvis, that's not what we're going to prescribe for you, and we don't want you taking anything else on top of this medication. We're trying to clear up your sinuses, your eyes.*"

It was a terrible thing and he was the victim of polypharmacy and malpractice by several doctors. I'm not so quick to condemn Dr. Kanoppolous, aka Dr. Nick—I like him—I liked his son, I think really Dr. Nick really meant to do the best he could for Elvis. And some of the other doctors that, well his dentist for instance, when he'd go to get a filling, they'd give him pain medication or something, 'cause when you have a root canal, you need that. Everyone does. But you take it the way it's prescribed. One tablet, with meals, before dinner, whatever. I don't know what the prescription is.

"Elvis always felt, as far as medications went, that more was better, so if one would make pain subside, certainly two or three would knock it out completely. So, he really shouldn't have been medicating himself. And that's nothing against Elvis, really, he just didn't know any better. And nobody would say no to him. They'd go and fill these prescriptions themselves and then bring it to him. And he had a regime of pills that apparently he would take before he went to bed, or get up, or whatever, but the key here is that he was in so much pain.

"And that we, I know all of us, would go to him.

"*Elvis, this next show, make an announcement, and say 'I'm tired. I'm going to take a year off.'*"

"I can't do that guys. The fans."

"*The fans will forgive you. You need a vacation. You need to rest. Go the beach. Buy a boat. Go deep-sea fishing. Take a year off* and get yourself back in fighting form. We don't want to see you like this. We don't want to see you this way. We love you. That's why we're talking to you."

"Guys, I can't do it. The Colonel's got all these tour schedules coming up that some of you may know and some of you may not know about. But I've got to do that."

"Elvis, we just told you that the fans will forgive you, if they even need to forgive you. Take a year off. Get some therapy. Get yourself fixed up. You're not a junkie, but get yourself weaned off that stuff. And then let's see if we can get you some specialists to see if they look at the things that have been diagnosed. Let's deal with your glaucoma with a specialist. Let's check out your bowel problems. A little surgery, maybe? Certainly within a year you'll be back to fighting form. And you'd feel better on stage."

"And he wouldn't do it because he felt that he would be letting his fans down, and that was what mattered to him: his fans. After all, they had gotten him to this level.

"*Johnny (without the fans), I wouldn't be nothing except for another damn lounge singer, in a bar with an acoustic guitar playing 'Love Me Tender.'*"

"So he didn't want to disappoint his fans. But he didn't realize he actually was disappointing them by not being able to take care of himself. He didn't realize that; we did, but he didn't.

"As far the pills, that's all I can say about it. I never saw him take anything more than an aspirin. And he didn't drink alcohol, except maybe on special occasions. I think up in the suite one time somebody, he wanted orange juice and told them to put something in there, and I think somebody put a drop and half of vodka in the glass and the rest was orange juice. And he drank about half of that and left that around. I think at dinner one night I think I saw him drink maybe a glass of wine, maybe a half. So, he wasn't a drinker. It was those damn prescription medications that did him in."

It was important to John to talk about this, especially from the historical standpoint that Elvis didn't take pills for recreation, but because he had physical problems that required medication rather than physical problems that were a result of drug abuse.

"There was no recreational drug use. He used them because he was exhausted, or one of the physical problems that he had flared up and they put him in the hospital. But he loved to go to Hawaii. He loved the beach and going swimming on those little paddleboat kinds of things. I think he, my personal opinion is that, yeah he did have a bit of a problem relaxing. He wanted people around that would relax with him, tell jokes, play music or something—he was restless. He didn't know how to, or he was unable to, know how to relax. Just relax or take it easy."

— 4 —

Although Elvis endured health problems until the end of his life, it's important to remember that Elvis remained Elvis, with plans for a long future and innovative career. Despite some erratic actions in some concerts or privately, John always enjoyed the company of his friend.

"Yes, there was a little abrupt behavior here and there," he says. "But overall, he was still the same Elvis. Talk to him, laugh with him, giggle with him."

John does explain an unfortunate experience that tries to be fair to both sides, involving an incident between Elvis and the Sweet Inspirations on stage.

"We were down in maybe North Carolina, the Carolinas, and keep in mind that Elvis would never intentionally disparage or hurt or embarrass anybody. He made a very unfortunate comment at the time that he thought was funny, and was meant to be heard only by people on stage, and certainly not by the audience.

"Well, the Sweets, they are black, and are very aware of the stereotypical portrayals of blacks, and Elvis made a comment walking by them.

"*You all been eating catfish or something? That breath. Catfish or watermelon or what?*"

"And that really ticked them off and unwisely, they chose to walk off the stage. And they took Kathy with them. And they walked off the stage, which was very unprofessional. It's always been my feeling that if you got a problem with your boss, no matter what your job is that you're doing, you don't discuss it there, you wait 'til after, you call the secretary or you call him up, and say, 'I need some time to talk with you. I got some real issues to discuss with you.'

"And in their case, they didn't do it and they walked off stage,

Guns, TVs and Bob Goulet

"Elvis had a thing about Robert Goulet. Bob Goulet is a nice fellow and a very good singer in my mind's eye. Everyone likes Goulet. Elvis had this thing, he felt Bob Goulet was copying his hairstyle, when actually the idea of jet black hair was from Tony Curtis; Elvis wanted to copy Tony himself!

"And he thought Bob Goulet was arrogant. By the way, Mr. Goulet was a real nice fellow, or at least he's always been nice to me. I don't know about anybody else's experiences with Mr. Goulet, but he's just a nice fella. And he'd see Bob Goulet on TV and for whatever reason in his mind, he'd snap, pull out a pistol and blow up the TV. He would also do that with newscasters, who would say, 'Is this the end of Elvis,' and say perhaps some negative things about him. Out would come the pistol, and BOOM, out would go the TV. He'd shoot 'em out in the hotels too.

"But he always replaced them. He would call down to the desk:

"My TVs broke, you guys send up another one?"

"And when they'd send it up, they'd see the TV:

"My God, what happened to the TV?"

"Well, it was an accident. Nothing serious. Just put that on my account and I'll pay for the new TV or whatever."

"So, it wasn't like the Rolling Stones who would go into the hotel and throw furniture out the window into a pool. Yeah, that was the only thing he ever destroyed. And there were a couple times when one of those bullets would go astray and almost hit somebody. Linda Thompson could tell you that she was in a suite up in the top of the Hilton. And she was in the bathroom and the restroom was right off the main room, and Elvis's gun went off unintentionally but the bullet went through the wall of the bathroom and came real close to hitting her. And it upset her. She came out. She had finished doing whatever she was doing, and she was pretty upset and scared.

"What was that? What happened? Who's shooting guns in here?"

"So we all left. We figured now's the time to exit. 'Cause he needed to do some explaining. Yeah, he'd blow out TVs. A way of releasing his frustrations, I think. Rather violently. But he never intentionally tried to hurt anybody or cause pain and destruction."

and threatened to leave the tour. They were going back to their homes and do whatever they were going to do. Back in L.A.

"Elvis I think instantly realized what he had said. He didn't have a prejudiced bone in his body. He grew up around blacks and black singers, guitar players and blues. He had a high degree of respect for those entertainers. Those people that actually gave him his start.

"And he knew instantly that he had made a bad faux pas. But that's all it was. It was an unintentional thing and it hurt the Sweets badly. They claimed it was just outright racial prejudice, and it certainly was not. It came off that way but it was not. And the newspapers picked it up too, that he had given his backup group the Sweet Inspirations, a real bad racial slap, and that's exactly how it translated to the audience and that's how it translated to the reporters there that saw how it happened.

"And to Elvis, it really shook him, and he did not intend for that to happen. It was a mistake, and he readily admitted it, and he caught the Sweets before they left and somebody told me he apologized profusely.

"I'm sorry. It was ill advised. I don't know why I said it. It was just something that I said that I thought was funny at the time. I know it was not funny and I shouldn't have said it."

"But they really still did hold it against him. And still threatened to leave. But they did come back. But he was very embarrassed by that."

John noticed around this time that Elvis's enthusiasm seemed to be fading. He recognized that his friend didn't seem to be into it like he ought to be and this was very difficult for John to observe.

"It was heartbreaking for me. I think a lot of that was brought on by the fact that he was bored. He wasn't having fun with his music anymore. He wasn't getting any really good material anymore to record and perform.

"Even 'Suspicious Minds' was getting to be old for him. He wasn't getting those big songs that we were talking about. He wanted to have those power songs to show his mature voice. He was getting bored with it. He wasn't having fun anymore. It was a job.

"And he felt the same way about performing music that I did that whenever it becomes a job, it's time to hang it up. He was just bored and looked weary. But that portion of it was because he was so sick that he desperately needed not to be performing. He needed to take a year off ... maybe two years. He wouldn't have been forgotten. He would've come back fresh and new again. But sadly he didn't do that and nobody seemed to push the issue further than that."

Good Vibrations

While the obstacles of lack of fresh material for Elvis to sing and health problems that he lived with daily were issues, the TCB Band continued to successfully tour and plenty of good times were had.

John recalls one funny incident involving a fan during a show in Las Vegas.

"Oh yes! In Las Vegas, this gal, probably 35, 40, she was there every night, front row center. It must've cost her a fortune to get that one seat, right there next to the stage. Her mouth was always open, just, 'Elvis, oh my God,' obviously not only a fan but in love, or in lust, hoping against hope that maybe he would recognize her or think to tell one of these guys, 'See that girl right down there. See if she wants to come up to the suite or something tonight.' Which is not terribly unusual.

"When 'Patch it Up' came along, she'd really get excited. And this particular night when the curtain came up and Elvis came out and was doing his show, we all saw her.

"Here she is again."

"But this gal, she was rocking with the music, back and forth, and 'Patch it Up' comes on, and she's really getting excited. And right at the end, she screamed and passed out. Just kaboom, face down in the guacamole. And we all noticed, and Elvis noticed too, and here come the hotel security guards 'cause people have been known to have heart attacks down there, or in the coffee shop after they lost a lot of money or something. And the fear was that maybe this gal had a heart attack or something, a stroke.

"So, these security guards come and get her and pull her up, and her dress was flipped up and she had this huge, big 12-inch vibrator still turned on, stuck right in her. She'd been using that thing all the way through 'Patch it Up' and she just had the most intense climax I guess and she got her wish.

"They carried her out of there. Fortunately, one of the security boys pulled her dress down and in a case like that I guess there's probably something in the law you can't touch something like that without a doctor present or a nurse present or something. I don't know what they did with her. They took her out of the showroom, that much I do know. It was incredible.

"We all knew and the girls, the Sweets, Kathy knew exactly what was happening and JD, the old lecher, he knew what was going on; we all knew. Good lord, Elvis. The things you do to these women."

Elvis fans love Elvis as much as one can love anyone without actually knowing him. And it is eternally frustrating for fans to know that Elvis was not being properly cared for during his health decline and that Elvis himself pushed himself inappropriately for his state of health.

Knowing this part of Elvis history makes any fan want to get into a time machine and take him aside and say, "Elvis please! Don't keep taking all this medication, take a rest, get healthy and then come sing again. Better to lose you for a year or two than lose you forever."

It's a constant question in everyone's mind: Why didn't someone really confront him and if people did, why didn't Elvis listen?

Meanwhile, Elvis Presley himself remained a frustrated musician due to lack of quality material coming his way. This was one of the stranger mysteries to John.

"He had plenty of friends in the business. And I'm sure he contacted them. On his own, not relying (just on others), knowing full well he couldn't rely on some of his people to go out and beat the bushes for new stuff. But there were plenty of good young writers around at that time that had good material that he could've done. They would've worked well on stage. I heard a lot of stuff out of Memphis, even up north ... sometimes after we'd get back to the hotel from the concert venue in some cities, some of us would go out to the local lounges where there was entertainment. We'd hear really good, local bands and singers.

"And there was a couple places where songwriters would debut their songs for the club audience. And we heard some wonderful songs and we'd talk to the writers.

"Are you looking to job your songs out to have people record them?"

"Well, yeah. That's what I'd like to do, eventually."

"Well, how would you feel about eventually getting one of your things to Elvis Presley?"

"Well, of course they'd be excited about that. Well, there was nothing we could do about that. We would take that information back to Joe or Lamar or somebody or Red:

"We heard this guy last night and he was doing some material

that was really nice stuff. Some good ballads, some things that could be power songs, if they were interpreted by Elvis."

"And we gave that information to Lamar or other people. And apparently, they didn't act on it or they figured that, 'no, if it didn't come from us then someone's going to lose a job.'

"Because they were on the dole anyways, some of these guys. But Elvis really expected and his experience was that songs were always given to him. Leiber and Stoller, people like that, were writing songs specifically for him. And sent it over to him on a demo. And they knew exactly what Elvis needed at that time. You pay people to do that kind of thing for you."

Another incident involved the famous wrought-iron gates at the entrance of Graceland, around 1974.

"We'd done a concert in Memphis with Elvis, and it was the first time he performed in Memphis in many, many years. And so it was like a hometown-boy-comes-home-and-does-good.

"'Cause we played Midsouth Coliseum, I guess it was. And he had invited us all back to Graceland, the orchestra, the band, the singers, everybody. Come back to Graceland and we'll chow down on potato chips and dip, Cokes and all that and have a good time.

"So, we all loaded on the bus that we would go to the various venues in and come to Graceland. And the bus driver called ahead to the gatehouse and asked them to open up the gates. Well, the bus driver pulled in but the right hand gate hadn't opened all the way. So, the bus pulls in there and we hear crunch, grind and scrape and the right gate fell off. And we went, 'Oh my word, the music gate!'

"The bus driver felt terrible. He stopped and got out and Vester says, 'Keep going. Don't worry about it. We'll get it fixed.' Bus driver came in and said, 'I'm really a better bus driver than that.'

"But it seemed so strange that as the bus had hooked the gate and was still moving forward, you could see the gate follow us and Marty Harrell was sitting right behind me. He was the lead trombone player in Guercio's orchestra.

"My God, that thing's following us!"

"He's hooked that gate and heard all the scrap. It came right off the hinges. By morning it was back functional and fixed."

Elvis strikes a pose as James Burton and John look on.

CHAPTER 13

Known Only to Him

— 1 —

By 1977, it became impossible for John and his fellow musicians not to be worried about their friend. John recalled something once that Elvis told him in a private conversation while watching their old friend, Duke, on TV:

"*I don't expect to live a long life. Who wants to see a 50-year-old Elvis?*"

"Everybody. We all grow older, and you've just gotten better with age. I mean your voice is terrific."

Still, those around Elvis could see by spring of '77 that he just wasn't Elvis.

"Not the Elvis we knew. We were terribly worried about him. It was obvious nothing was being done for him, constructive in any way. Now he was not having fun on stage, and that last tour, the final tour, we should never have gone on. We should have not done that. It should've been postponed so he had a chance to rest.

"And get himself hydrated again. We saw signs of dehydration, and it was obvious he couldn't see very well, 'cause of the glaucoma. And he had to leave the stage a couple times because he was drinking so much water and Gatorade that he had to leave and go to the bathroom.

"He was in terrible shape, and we could see this. And his jumpsuit wasn't fitting him right; he just looked flat awful. And all of our hearts went out to him.

"What's happened here? What can we do?"

"Well, there was nothing we could do that we hadn't already tried. All of us would've given any amount of time if there was something that needed to be done to turn him around. By April '77, it was really obvious and to most of us:

"Boy, he hasn't got long."

"Kathy and myself, said, 'Well, he said he didn't expect to live long.' 'Course his mother died when she was 42, and he was 42. It was just so painfully obvious—not only to us, 'cause we were real close to him, but to the audience.

"But the reaction to his performances was still the same. They were still screaming and yelling and the flash bulbs were still going off all around the arena. From their standpoint, it didn't seem like they were seeing anything but of course they did. They had to. Even when his body was finally giving up on him and was just shutting down, he still never lost that marvelous voice.

"But that's a tour that never should have happened. He never looked worse. There was an obvious yellow tinge around him that I suspected was jaundice of some sort. He had come to terms with the way he looked. But he still didn't feel good. He was having trouble breathing … it was like a labor of love for him to be on that stage anymore."

The Colonel arranged for a CBS special consisting of footage shot over the course of several concerts on this tour. Fans familiar with this show are well aware that the appearance of Elvis betrayed his declining health.

"The '77 Special was filmed in Omaha and Sioux Falls, South Dakota, I think. There's footage of all the other cities that fans took (of that tour). I haven't seen it. And if you see the last tour, you'll see he's just ragged. But still that marvelous voice never gave up on him. He felt so bad although the shows were quite good."

— 2 —

"The last time I saw him, was the last concert of that tour, June 26, 1977, (which happened to be Colonel's birthday by the way) in

Indianapolis at the Market Square Arena. That's the last concert he ever did.

"The show went very well and he sounded great and the audience reacted beautifully, as I remember it. And then we were supposed to start a new tour in August, August 16th, in Portland, Maine. And the way it worked was all the Los Angeles-based talent would go to LAX or Burbank International. We would all travel on our show plane, which was a big Elektra jet 99, four-propeller thing, Holiday Airlines, that they rented for all the crew and equipment.

"We had real nice flight attendants on there that took good care of us. Those were wonderful gals, too. We all boarded the plane. What we would do was leave Los Angeles and fly to Las Vegas, and get all the Vegas-based people, being Joe Guercio's orchestra, without the string people. And then we would leave Las Vegas and head to the next venue. Our destination was Portland, Maine.

"We got Joe and his guys, and we were heading for Portland, and it wasn't very long—we were over Colorado—the pilot came on the intercom.

"*Ladies and Gentleman: We need to set the plane down here in Colorado and check the plane.*"

"And to me, it seemed very strange because the plane could go from coast to coast with no stops. But then again, if we had to set the plane down, there had to be a good reason. I figured chances are there's nothing wrong with the plane but it had to do with communications.

"He set down in Pueblo, Colo., on a far-away runway. And he came in the cabin.

"*We're going to be here just a little bit. So why don't you stretch out a bit on the tarmac, runway, for a little bit. We got a long flight to Portland.*"

So we got out. And one of the flight officials at the airport there came running over.

"*Is Marty here?*"

"*I'm Marty, what's up?*"

"We were very concerned for Marty and his family, thinking

John gives Elvis a Guitar

In John's basement there sits a beautiful acoustic guitar that he had custom made for Elvis. Here, he recounts the bittersweet story of that guitar.

"Elvis at the time, about 1973, was showing some strange behavior on stage. He was frustrated and I know part of the reason was he wasn't getting the material he wanted to record and perform on stage. And he broke a couple of guitars, acoustic guitars during performance. And that wasn't like him. He wasn't like some of those bands that set fire to their guitars. He threw one or two out into the audience after they were destroyed.

And I thought once again, just like when I met him in Springfield, 'The boy ain't having any fun. Something's wrong here. I know my thoughts. I thought, he's giving and giving and giving to everybody. I don't recall anyone giving him anything.'

"I tell you what. I wasn't looking for brownie points or anything, 'maybe I should get him a little something.' If he had his own guitar, his very own guitar, something he could hold precious to him, even though he still couldn't play very well ... he knew E and A and that other chord (B7)!

"So, I called a guy down in Tennessee, the Gallagher Guitar Company and talked to Bill Gallagher himself.

"Bill, this is John Wilkinson."

"Oh, Hi John, how you doing?"

"OK, fine. I want you to build me a guitar, Bill and I want it to be the most beautiful, the best guitar you've ever turned out of your factory.

"OK, what do you want on it?"

"I want mother-of-pearl abalone, three-piece back, striped like the D-series Martins and on the fingerboard, I want 'Elvis Presley' put on there and on the peghead I want the TCB logo. And on the bridge I want EP. And I want it to be the best guitar you ever made."

"John, I knew it wasn't for you when you started talking about the abalone and all that. They're priced about right, expensive but worth it. John, this ain't gonna be cheap."

"That was in first of '74. It took him three years to build it. At the beginning of '77, Bill came out to L.A. He called me.

"John, Bill Gallagher. I've got your guitar. I'm here for a meeting."

"Bill, Jesus! OK! I'll bring my checkbook!"

"So, I get to his hotel and he fixes me a drink in his room and he opens this guitar case and shows me the most incredible looking guitar I've ever seen in an acoustic. It turned out exactly like I wanted it. The action, you have to string with telephone cables just about because Elvis didn't play a guitar but when he did, he beat it so the action is up. I looked it over, played it a little bit.

"This is exactly what I was looking for, thank you, Bill."

"That'll be $5,000."

"At that time, that was a lot of money for a guitar. Now, it's about right for a high-end Gibson. I wrote him a check.

"I took the guitar home because I had to get ready for another tour. And that turned out to be the last tour Elvis ever did, June 1977. So I took it with me and I wanted the opportunity to give it to him but I wanted it to be one on one like our private conversations, like we had all those years.

"Well, that opportunity didn't present itself until June 26, 1977, in Indianapolis at the Market Sqauare Arena, which is the last show we ever did.

"I was onstage tuning my guitar and Charlie's and Elvis's, and I saw the limo and saw him go in the dressing room, and I thought, 'This is it.'

"I finished my job making sure all the guitars were tuned and I went off the stage and I got the guitar case, and I went up to his dressing room door and knocked. Sam Thompson opened it.

"Hi Johnny, how you doing?"

"Fine, can I talk to Elvis for a minute?"

"Is anything wrong?"

"No, no, not at all."

"Come on in."

"There was only Sam, Vernon and Elvis in the room. Elvis was in another portion of the room putting on his stage clothes. He came out.

"Hey John, what's going on? Everything OK?"

"Everything's just fine, boss, have a seat on the couch there."

"What?"

"Sit down!"

"OK, what's up?"

"I put the guitar case up on the coffee table in front of the couch."

"That's yours. Open it up."

"What?"

"He opened it up and his eyes got big.

"That's a beautiful guitar. It's got my name on it and everything."

"That's it. That's your guitar, man. You have given and given and given until there's nothing left to give for everybody, and you've done worlds for my career and I don't recall a time that anyone's given you something. I'm not looking for brownie points or anything Elvis, I just felt in my heart I wanted to give you something, something special to you from me, that's all. Pick that guitar out of that case, put a strap on there and see how it feels."

"He put it on, he had on his show belt and all that. He never used it on stage, unfortunately. He put it on and strummed that E and that A but didn't get to that other chord.

"This is beautiful, Johnny, it's almost too beautiful. I'm afraid I'll wreck it."

"Wreck it, throw it away, use it for kindling, whatever you want, it's your guitar, it's a gift from me to you."

"I'll tell you what, Johnny. You take this guitar, take it home with you, and I'll let you know when I need it again. OK? It's beautiful, thank you very much."

"He gave me a hug.

"It's gorgeous, thank you very much."

"So, I put it back in the case and locked it up and put it with the other guitars and took it home with me. Of course, he never called for it again because he shuffled off this mortal coil a couple of months later."

Did it hurt John's feelings that Elvis didn't keep it right then?

"No, no, I think he was in shock that somebody had actually given him something of worth. Not just going to the store and buying him something fun for Christmas but actually went and had something made specifically for him that was his and for nobody else."

something had happened. He went with this official, who said there was a message for him at this control tower. So Marty went. We watched where he went and made sure he got there OK.

"Well, he came back about 10 minutes later, as white as a ghost. He was always happy-go-lucky. He climbs to the top of the stairs to board the plane.

"*I got terrible news. It's all over. We're going home. Elvis died this morning.*"

"And of course, we all just started crying.

"*What? Elvis Presley just doesn't die. He gets sick, but he doesn't die. He's the King of Rock 'n' Roll.*"

"*That's the word. I'm sorry. We're all going home. The plane has been instructed to turn around and go to Las Vegas and then Los Angeles.*"

"So, the officials who had taken Marty stood around and said, 'Any of you who want to call your relatives or wives, husbands, please come with us.' So, I went and had to call my girlfriend at the time. And of course, she had heard because it had broken through all the airwaves. And the newspapers had already begun making their headlines. It was a tough day. And there was dead silence on the plane. No card games. No jokes. We were all just sitting there. We realized it was the end of the era."

"So, we dropped off Joe and his guys.

"*We'll all be in touch. This does not mean the end of our relationships.*"

"And we got to L.A. and hugged and shook hands.

"*See you all. I'm sure we'll all get together again and do something.*"

"And eventually, we did. I remember my girlfriend had pulled up, along with my dog, well her dog—but he liked me better!—Murphy, who by the way, is the dog that I named my Gibson Crest after, which is Mr. Murphy.

"And Murphy came up and gave me dog licks, because he knew something, 'cause mommy was very upset too. He was jumping all over everyone trying to cheer everyone up. But we all got in our cars and went home, 'cause it was the end. We all knew it was the end.

"And still to this day, it seems to me, sometimes it still doesn't set in. I mean, I know he's gone, but right immediately after I got home, I decided I needed to go back to Memphis. And I called and chartered a plane to Memphis and I disguised myself and put on an old baseball cap and old work jeans and dark glasses—nobody recognized me.

"I went to Memphis and checked in the Howard Johnson motel, which is kinda near Graceland, and called the house, and one of the cooks answered and she knew who I was. I asked for Vernon, and he got on the phone, Elvis's daddy.

"Vernon, this is John Wilkinson. I'm in Memphis. I came to see if there's anything I can do to help; run errands, help. I just wanted you to know I'm here."

"I did go to the funeral. No one recognized me. Well, Kathy recognized me. And JD.

"John, is that you? You don't look so good."

"Are any of us looking that good?"

"I was there for the funeral and Rex Humbard, the Reverend. Very nice gentleman and was close to Elvis. Kathy sang and JD and the boys sang, favorites of Elvis. It was hard to believe, looking at him in the box. It didn't seem real. But it was him. All that talk of it being a wax dummy, or there being an air conditioner unit in the bottom of the casket, total bullshit. That's just the tabloids trying to keep the thing alive when it was obviously over.

"Afterward, we filed around and I kissed him on the cheek, and it was him. And Charlie, earlier in the day, had trimmed his sideburns and cut his hair, and he looked real nice, just fine. I would have rather seen him standing up, but …

"They let some fans in and they filed along and paid their respects to their idol. That was a sad time, a sad August. Still to this day, August 16, and November 22, are two very tough days for me. And June 6, when Bobby Kennedy was assassinated. I campaigned for him on the train, singing with him with John Stewart, so I lost some really good friends. It's still a very tough time. My friend was gone. I think Bill Medley summed it up best in a song he released called 'Old Friend:'

"*Would you still be here if I could've been there?*"

"Well, no is the answer, but he loved Elvis. And Elvis felt the same about Bill. And what's not to love about Bill Medley? Bill Medley is a gentleman, a wonderful person and has time for everybody. He loved Elvis. And not only had they had a mutual respect for one another, but a real mutual friendship.

"That's when all the tabloids came out and mentioned all the Elvis sightings, that he faked his death. Well, some people believe that. But you had to know Elvis, and know that as he had a reputation as a practical joker, he would never go *that* far with a practical joke. He wouldn't do that to his daddy, who was in ill health, or to his fans. We knew because we saw the deterioration from '74 until his death. I think we all felt deep down that he's not long for this world, unless something drastic is done to help him. I think we all felt a curtain coming down.

"Through it all, like the lyrics in the song, he did it his way. Elvis Presley, boy. What a deal. I never expected in my born days—except in my childhood dreams—that I would be a part of his life."

John again reminds the fans that despite deteriorating health, Elvis was by no means looking at his life as over during that

Look, Ma: Elvis!

"My mom and dad went to a concert in Springfield, Mo., on the last tour. They didn't meet Elvis but I was able to secure nice seats for them on my right side, and they could see him when he came out the tunnel when he climbed to the stage.

"And afterward, my folks said 'thank you for the tickets. Great show.' And of course, when Elvis introduced me in my hometown, the place came unglued. And when he announced this, Elvis said:

"Did you bring your mom and dad, John?"

"As a matter of fact I did Elvis. There they are."

"And my parents waved at Elvis. After the show they asked:

"He's not feeling well, is he John?"

"No, he isn't. He's not the Elvis I signed up with."

"He was just in terrible condition. Again, though, I emphasize that his voice was just incredible. He did 'My Way' and 'American Trilogy'—he was right in there."

period. On the contrary and as always, Elvis looked forward to the future.

"Everyone assumes that he was so depressed, he's not singing right, he's gonna give it up. In actuality, he had a lot of plans. He wanted to do movies, not just in the acting role but he wanted to get behind the camera as a director, perhaps. The karate film never transpired but he sunk a lot of money into it at the behest of people. I think there's some footage somewhere but I haven't seen it surface. It might not exist.

"He had lots and lots of plans and if he was depressed at all it was because he was in such pain. His body was giving out on him. His mind wasn't. He was constantly thinking."

John waves to his fans after a performance.

CHAPTER 14

Performing for the Fans

— 1 —

AFTER ELVIS PASSED, AS MIGHT BE EXPECTED, music no longer appealed to John as a career.

"I decided that I didn't really want to do music anymore because music just didn't mean anything anymore. Without Elvis, there was just no reason to play music. Well, my buddies didn't see it quite that way. They could see not playing music, but not doing anything was putting me downhill too. They wouldn't let that happen.

"John, I know a couple of guys who want to be in a band and have you as the lead singer out in front. What do you say?"

"Well, OK."

"And they were friends with a guy who owned a club down in El Segundo, called the Skylark. And they invited the owner from the Skylark up to the drummer's house where we were rehearsing and he said 'You're hired.' We had all these sets put together, five or six different sets, and played there for two-and-a-half years. And I was back in music. It felt good. This was '80 through '83. After I got married, that was it. I didn't play with them anymore, or in L.A.

"And also during that time, I wanted to expand my horizons a little bit since I more or less decided I didn't want to do music anymore. I took a job at Radio Shack. And why, I don't know. I wanted something to do. I was so used to working with Elvis and my salary was excellent. But I wanted something to do. I just didn't want to sit around and all day at home because if I did I would just get all glum about Elvis.

"So, I took a job with Radio Shack and wound up climbing the corporate ladder to where I was managing four stores in the Los Angeles area. And I'm proud to say all four of those stores had the best bottom line of any in California. And I worked my people, and I worked them hard. I said, 'This is the only way you're going to go anywhere.' And several of my employees went on to be managers and a couple I think went on to where they had their own franchise. So I worked for Radio Shack for three or four years."

John left Radio Shack due to several armed robberies and the fact that corporate would not allow its employees to arm themselves. John next worked for Hughes Aircraft for seven and half years.

"I fully intended to put in 20 years and retire like anybody else would retire after 20 years. And I climbed the corporate ladder. I was forced out of the company, due to my stroke. I was a supervisor, making supervisor status, and I had 18 people working under me. And I did real well. The employees liked me; the upper management liked me. And I straightened out a lot of things so when the Air Force came by to do audits, our records were clean as a whistle. And they could check anything they wanted to."

— 2 —

John met Terry Cottrell in the late '70s while Terry was dating his roommate and stopped by one day to find he wasn't home but John was. They watched TV for awhile, struck up a friendship and eventually started dating. They married July 16, 1983.

Through the 1980s, John continued to enjoy success in the "real world," as his accomplishments at Radio Shack and Hughes show. At the end of the decade, he got a surprise phone call.

"In 1989, I had vacation time coming. And James Burton had called me, it was a Friday.

"*Hey John. James Burton here.*"

"*Hey J.B., how ya doing?*"

"We talked for a minute.

"Look, there's a fellow over in Switzerland that wants to do some Elvis shows, and he wants to hire the TCB Band. Bring us over and we'll be over there for a week. We're going to do five shows in five different cities."

"OK. Are these Elvis impersonators you're talking about J.B.?"

"Yeah, but I hear he's really good."

"OK. But he's not Elvis."

The impersonator actually hired the TCB Band to back him. John's opinion of his abilities is not very positive but the pay was right.

"He went into hock, up way past his neck to make this happen for him. So we did that. We went to Switzerland and played all five shows. Kathy was with us and JD and the boys, and the five TCB Band members. And we tried to make this kid look good but no matter what you did, you couldn't make this kid look good. He was just too bad. And we all felt like:

"Where did you try to think you could do Elvis?"

"We told him not to quit his day job. Because you're not going to be making a living doing this. And then we came home, flew back, and we were all tired. Because that was a real whirlwind tour; five different cities, five different shows, it was all by bus. I got home on April 14, which is my wife's birthday, and we got home and I dropped my suitcases and said, 'I gotta go to bed.'

"Well, we were supposed to go down to her sister's place because my sister-in-law's daughter had the same birthday as Terry, April 14. Well, we weren't going to make it that day but go down the next day. And that next morning, I woke around 3:30 in the morning, and I was hungry. So, I fixed a bowl of cereal, and some milk, maybe some grapefruit, I don't know. And I ate, I felt fine. I went back to bed. About 7:00 a.m., I got up, April 15, 1989, tax day ...

"I woke up and I thought, 'well, I better get up, get cleaned.'

"Well, I tried to get up but I couldn't do it: My left side didn't work. So, I thought, 'I've been sleeping on my arm.' You sleep crooked, and the blood stops, then you're able to make it work again.

"I was on my way to the bathroom to shower and shave and all that, and Terry comes around the corner and takes one look at me.

"Johnny, you've had a stroke."

"What? You gotta be crazy."

"No, go look in the mirror."

"So I did, and she went and called a doctor, and I looked in the mirror and the whole left side of my face was hanging down. And I knew then, that I'd been hit. But at that time, my left arm hadn't been working. I couldn't open my left hand.

"Oh no, that's my guitar hand."

"Terry had called our family doctor and he had told her to get me right down to the emergency room at the Hospital Marina Del Ray, and that he'd be waiting for us. And I was ready to drive down there myself. My wife took my keys and we took our neighbor went with us.

"Terry drove me down there and they were waiting, and put me in the gurney. They wheeled me up into the emergency room and ran tests, they did a cat scan and an MRI and whatever they did, and put me on life-sustaining fluids and found I had a stroke. But my face had almost come back, so I thought, 'Hey my face is coming back, my arm could come back.' It didn't work that way.

"They didn't have the kind of things that they have today. Had they been able to give me a certain type of medication within the hour, well then maybe, paralysis wouldn't have happened. They found an aneurism in my brain about the size of a golf ball. It hadn't burst, thankfully, because it would've drowned me and killed me.

"So, they immediately put me in a room, with IVs all over the place, and catheters here and catheters there, and our family doctor came in and we were glad to see him—a wonderful man—Dr. Newfield. I'll never forget him.

"It's serious business, John. Here's what's happened: You had an aneurism and stroke. The aneurisms were right on the motor strip that controls the right and left side of your body."

"And basically it affected my left side. My speech was fine, and I didn't go blind or anything, so right then I thought, 'I'm lucky.' I have seen what a stroke can do.

"I don't know what we're going to do about it. I'm calling in a couple of specialists down in Louisiana, or somewhere. There are a couple brain surgeons who are well known for this kind of thing. They're going to fly in and take a look. And then we'll make a decision on what we're going to do."

"They had several ways in which they could go: It all involved surgery. They could go in and clip it off, or take it out, or do it through oral meds and injections, and finally these two fellows came in and they were reassuring.

"What we're going to do is split your head, like a melon, and go in there and take that aneurism out. Try to hook you back up. We can't give you a real good guarantee of how it's going to turn out but if we don't do this you will surely die."

"So, they gave me less than a 2-percent chance to survive the surgery. They shaved off all my rock 'n' roll hair and got me prepped. It took them 13 hours, and Terry was there and a lot of friends that she had told. And right in the middle of that surgery there was an earthquake in Los Angeles. That scared them out of the waiting room. All they could see in there were these instruments scrambling my brains like someone would be scrambling eggs. But fortunately, all the equipment and instruments are on rollers, and the operating rooms are on rollers, so it absorbed the impact of the earthquake.

"It shook up the city but it didn't do a whole lot of damage and fortunately, it didn't do any damage to the hospital or me. But Terry told me later a nurse came running out.

"*He's OK, he's OK. Everything's on rollers. Nothing happened.*"

"But it took them 13 hours to pull that aneurism out of there and to stitch me back up. You can still see a scar here where they cut my head open. I'll tell you what, I had the worst headache afterward. They put me in ICU.

"*I can take care of this if you give me some whiskey.*"

"No wonder I had a headache. It took a long time and I went to therapy and all that. But there was nothing there that they could do."

Before going to the hospital, the full effects of the stroke had not taken hold.

"I tried to get dressed at home to go to the hospital. I put on a shirt and my left hand wouldn't work. I couldn't get up there to button the shirt like you could normally. So, by that time, the full effects of the stroke, at most had taken place on the extremity anyways, I couldn't get out of the car to get on the gurney. It had paralyzed my left side.

"Over the next 90, days they kept me in the hospital, they transferred me to another hospital, and another neurologist, and this guy has no bedside manner, whatsoever. I had no faith or confidence in him. I wanted out of there so bad because I thought he was going to kill me. And I really thought so because I don't think he knew what he was doing, I think.

"He was a certified neurologist—he had the paper on the wall that said so—but what an asshole. I had monumental arguments with him. I threatened to drop him a couple of times. The stroke left me where there's like a separation of the shoulder. Well, he picked my arm up and shot it straight to the ceiling to see the range of motion and it hurt my arm, it really hurt. I didn't lose any sensation with the stroke, I just lost my motor function.

"I'd done some reading, in ICU in my private room, and I got some friends to bring me books on strokes and the effects of what can happen. I got to reading and I got to be pretty knowledgeable about it.

"Nothing you can do is going to make this arm come back. And I don't care about my leg. All I care about is my arm and hand so I can play the guitar."

"That's not going to happen, Johnny, I'm sorry. This is permanent paralysis."

"And it has turned out to be. But, also, I have, it was like a bolt of lightning that hit me, I realized if I concentrate on what I've lost, then I've really lost. But if I concentrate on what I have left, maybe there's still something there.

"So, I started singing in my room and I realized I could still speak, I could still sing, so OK. Any my buddies Don, other people came by for me and played piano or guitar so I could sing. Don took me up to the mountains for a gig; he taught me some right-hand piano, so I got along all right. It has not been an easy go for me since 1989 until the present time.

"But thanks to my friends who stuck by me and continued to believe in me and reassure me, and making me feel like I wanted to get going, I'm able to travel and the fan clubs want me—over in Europe especially—and I do some traveling in the United States to raise money for certain things, to sing."

— 3 —

After learning again to walk and care for himself, John's career became being John Wilkinson, former rhythm guitarist for Elvis Presley, and singer. John quickly became in demand by the legion of Elvis fans throughout the world.

"There's a couple, Ralph and Terry Foster, I need to mention them, who own a company called King Tracks, and the word had gotten around all over the world about what had happened to me and they had heard about it too.

"We had moved here to Sandy, Utah, and I was sitting in my office, and the phone rang.

"*John, this is Ralph Foster. I don't think you know me.*"

"No, I don't think I recognize your name right away, sir. What can I do for you?"

"And he told me about his company. They make minus tracks (recordings of Elvis songs without vocals) for Elvis impersonators.

"*What we want to do is we know you sing, we've gotten the word. We want to send you a complete collection of everything that we've recorded in minus tracks and let you try them out in some places, at parties or whatever, and sing against these tracks. And so you can get back into it. We want you back on stage.*"

"Well, I started doing that around here. Graceland, at the time, we were still friends, called.

"*There's some fan clubs that want to get a hold of you, John. Is it alright if we give them your phone number and address?*"

"*Yes, that's fine.*"

"So, I got calls from fan clubs here in the States and then the first cards and letters wishing me well and fast recovery came from Europe, and the first ones come from Belgium.

"So, I have a very close relationship with the Belgium fan clubs and the fans there. And Jacques Delessert, who had put together the TCB thing with that lame Elvis impersonator, called.

"*We've got a thing going here for Kaiserslauten, Germany. There's an Elvis impersonator. We got Kathy Westmoreland, JD Sumner and the Stamps and the Jordanaires, and we had a little band and they want you to get on stage and sing.*"

"Yeah, you betcha I can."

"So, I went over there and that's where I met Peter Verbruggen the first time. He had heard there was going to be this gathering of Elvis people performing for the first time together aside from the TCB and his newspaper sent him to this thing to write about it.

"We were staying at this hotel, in this real old castle, about a 1,000-year-old castle and we were down in the dining room area, talking amongst ourselves, the Jordanaires, I was talking to my friend Ray Walker. And this pleasant looking fellow, this giant guy, comes over and nobody was talking to me, as always—the mystery guy—and they served us this wonderful German wine, and this fellow came up.

"*Mr. Wilkinson? Hi, my name is Peter Verbruggen. I'm from old Belgium, and my newspaper has sent me. I'm a journalist for the biggest-circulated paper in Belgium. My paper sent me here because they know I'm an Elvis fan to cover this event with all these people that worked with Elvis on stage. I was wondering if I could do a little interview with you.*"

"We were all tired because we had just gotten in.

"*Surely Mr. Verbruggen, I would like to do that.*"

"*Please call me Peter.*"

"*I will if you call me John, Johnny or Hey You.*"

"We shook hands.

"*All right, John, how about—well, you're tired. Why don't you sleep in and come down to this little café that's on the other side of this dining room and meet me there about 1:30 or 2:00, we'll have lunch."*

"So Peter, bless his heart, has become a lifelong friend for me, like the brother I never had. Just like how I felt about Elvis. And I joined him at the table and I ordered up some stuff for us, we ate and talked, and he asked me about Elvis and our experiences together.

"Well, I got what I need. I'm going to come see the show tonight at the Barbaroso Hall, where you guys are going to perform. Before I leave here, would you do me a favor? My wife works for the local radio station in my home town of Mol. Would you do a couple of radio promos for me? You know what those are, right?"

"Sure, yeah."

"What's the numbers of the radio station?"

"It's 107.1 FM Radio Mol."

"So, I did a couple of those for him.

"Your home for the greatest golden oldies," and *"All the Elvis you can handle all day long,"* *"107.1 boys and girls. That's where you want to weld your radio to."*

"He took that back him with him. After the show, before he left to go back to Belgium, he asked:

"Would you give any consideration into coming to my home town to give a show?"

"I'd love to."

"Peter was the first to get me to come to Europe, to come and perform alone.

"Now, you have minus tracks?"

"Yes, I have those."

"Well, I have a friend that's a wonderful musician, that's a hell of a guitar player and why don't we see if I can put together a band for you to play behind you."

"I would much rather work with a live band. Because if I do something I can always blame it on the band. But with the minus track, there's no one to stand behind you and take the blame."

"We made an agreement on that and he told me about one of Belgium's own famous singers.

"We have a very famous singer in Belgium, our first lady of country music. Her name is Barbara Dex. And we think it would be really neat to have a concert featuring both of you. Ms. Dex would do a show and you would do a show, and then maybe the couple of you could do some songs together. We think this would be a huge draw."

"Peter, if you think so, then I'm all for it."

"I'll fly you over here and put you in a nice motel in Mol, which is a city of about 3,000 people."

"It's just gorgeous. Very nice people, very quaint. Just lovely. He brought me over there and put me in this nice motel and first time I was there, he took me over to his house and his wife fed me and they didn't have the kids yet. And then I went back to the hotel and got some much-needed sleep, and the next day, Peter called.

"I'll pick you up at noon and take you over to the convention center where you and Ms. Dex will perform."

"Wonderful complex, acoustics are amazing. After we toured the facility over there at the cultural center, Peter took me to meet the band.

"So, we go went back to my hotel and there's a lovely little bar over there with sandwiches, drinks, beer, whatever you want. We were waiting there, and in walks this real nice fellow, kinda skinny, tall, very pleasant face. I stood up of course, and Peter said, 'John, this is Geert.' We shook hands and sat down and we started talking, and they said more of the guys were coming in that they wanted me to meet. Good.

"And in walked my drummer, Danny Arnout, wonderful drummer. He's like those fellows in that documentary from Motown ("Standing in the Shadows of Motown"), he plays so well, just lays a beautiful foundation—no flashy drums. And his styles aren't loud and louder, it's taste and tastier. He's a pleasant young man and we talked.

"And fortunately all these people understand and speak English very well. So, there wasn't a problem with me understanding them and vice versa. And next walked in the bass player, Cyril Soul. Very distinguished looking man: white, combed-back hair and he was in a suit with a tie. He was actually a classical musician, but when Geert told him what he had in mind for a band with John Wilkinson, he jumped at the chance.

"So, Cyril sat down and we shook hands and talked, got to know everybody. The lead guitar player, he was a real flake. He didn't last long. Stefan thought it was his show, costarring the Ms. TCB Band and myself, and he had to be straightened out about that. But anyway, I met all these guys, and we talked and Geert said,

"You sent a list of the songs you wanted to do and we think we got it down pretty good but we want to hold two rehearsals with you so we make sure."

"Fine with me. You'll have to talk to Peter about scheduling because I don't know what's expected of me while I'm here. Do I have to talk with the fans? Or am I supposed to do some radio and TV?"

"I still hadn't met Ms. Barbara Dex. That night, Peter had set up a press conference for the TV, local television and national television was there also. Newspaper, radio people were there to ask questions. That's when I met Barbara. What a sweet lady. She comes walking in, blonde, rather big-boned girl, but she came up and was just so shy.

"You're John Wilkinson?"

"Yes, honey, I'm John Wilkinson. You're Barbara. May I call you Barbara?"

Her father was with her and he's a very famous folk singer in Belgium. He had quite a few albums out many years ago and a sweetheart of a guy. So, we went down and Barbara was right next to me, and whoever was directing the press conference said:

"Are you kids ready?"

"Kids? She's the kid ... I'm ready, are you ready, Barbara?"

"Yes, I'm ready, John (very solemnly)."

"Well, don't make it sound like an execution, honey. They ain't going to hurt us and they ain't even going to try. I'll take care of ya."

"The question-and-answer thing began and they asked if this was my first time in Belgium.

"In this capacity, yes. But I've been here in 1954 and 1960, not *in this city but in the country. And my parents brought me over on a vacation but I don't remember a whole lot about all that. I think we were just in Brussels."*

"How do you feel about working with Barbara's TCB Band?"

"I'm loving it. She's a songbird, guys, she's a songbird. And she's pretty as a picture, what can I say? This is going to be a really good concert."

When that was over Barbara gave me a hug.

"We're rehearsing tomorrow, don't you know?"

"I know, I know. Don't worry about it hon, I ain't going to hurt ya."

"So, anyhow, Geert's wife at the time, Karen, was one of the back-up singers, and another little girl, Mirjam, was the soprano and Ms. Dex insisted on being part of the back up group. Here she is very famous in Belgium and she wanted to be part of the back-up group? So, we rehearsed and we were very tight.

"Well, I opened up with Elvis's song, 'Let's Have a Party,' 'cause people like to rock and roll, moving and grooving. I did 'Early Morning Rain,' of course and 'Can't Help Falling in Love with You.' A bunch of the songs that Elvis was best known for and Barbara did some of the Elvis songs, too.

"Now, this just terrified the hell out of her because she claimed that she didn't know English very well. But I'm here to tell you that she speaks very, very fine English and understands it just fine, too. She had nothing to worry about but she was very concerned. She learned a bunch of Elvis songs, in English, to sing. She was used to singing in her native language, of Dutch, or Flemish. Now, this girl just tore those people apart, man. She sang so well and it was kinda odd to hear a female doing Elvis songs but she had them down. She growled when she was supposed to. The audience was just mesmerized. She opened the show and they just loved her as I expected they would because she was very famous with the Belgian people and of course her father, Mark Dex and his fame.

"So, it was my turn and I came out and did my thing and Barbara came out and we did 'Love Me Tender,' and the audience went just nuts. They really enjoyed seeing the two of us together and knowing full well that we had never met one another or worked together before and everything went smoothly. Wasn't any sour notes or anything.

"We're laughing and giggling and singing and the audience loved it. Thanks to Peter Verbruggen for getting me started back on stage as an out-front singer. Had it not been for Peter, I would probably not have done it over there. And one invitation followed another. That concert was so successful that Peter decided we should do another one. And in two years' time, same band, and Ms. Dex. She's now married and has a beautiful little baby boy and she's a perfect mother.

"So, we did the second concert there. Well, we did two shows on two successive days the first time. Then the second time we did two shows on the same day; a matinee and an evening. And the same reaction.

"By this time the word—now there was a lot of people from other countries that came to see these shows. And the word spread to Germany and France and Norway, Sweden, Denmark, all this ... and the offers started rolling in.

"*We want John to come over here and entertain us. He loves the fans. We've heard how he interacts with the fans.*"

"So, I started going. It's hard for me to travel long distances. It takes a lot out of me emotionally and physically—but I love doing it. I love doing it. I've been doing that ever since. For 27 years now. Going at least twice a year over to Europe and entertain the fans there. Give autographs ... the way they see me is not only as a performer, but as a last living link between themselves and their late idol, Elvis.

"They've learned that I don't gloss over anything. I tell the truth. And they're glad of that. Because they've heard enough guff and bullshit from the tabloids or Graceland and that's one of the reasons Graceland doesn't like me much. One of the reasons Graceland doesn't like me much is because they know I tell fans the truth. I don't sugarcoat anything. And the fans like me also because I don't charge an arm and leg for them to come see me. I try to keep my prices real low so anyone that wants to come see me can and not break up their weekly budget so they can keep food on their table for the family. And that's important to me too: I want all fans who want to come see me to be able to.

"And I'm treated like royalty over there, it's just amazing. You would think I was Elvis with the treatment I get. I can't take two steps out of my hotel room.

"*Mr. Wilkinson, do you need any food or anything? Do you need a ride some place?*"

"They have over there, what I like to call, something, sadly lacking in the United States today and has been for quite some time: old-world courtesy. They treat you as they would like to be treated. With courtesy and respect. And it's not hard to return that. And I still adhere to the way I always was. 'Yes, sir,' 'No, ma'am,' and I'm not trying to be cutesy-folk, fool ol' country boy. This is me, John Wilkinson. And that reputation got around too.

"*John is nice, John is approachable, and he'd be glad to talk to you and be decent to you.*"

"And I have yet to hear from any fan who feels like I disrespected them. During the 27 years that Elvis has been gone, I have been going overseas or here in the United States. Some of the fan clubs put shows together to benefit charity. Special Olympics and Breast Cancer Research are two of my favorites. And the club in Indianapolis each year holds two events that all the proceeds go to the Special Olympic athletes/kids.

"And then there's a group in Ohio and in Pittsburgh that raises money for the Breast Cancer Research Foundation people, which is extremely important to me because my own wife had breast cancer and subsequently lost her breast to it. And thankfully, she's free and clear of cancer, and she's fine. The only thing wrong is she has to put up with me. But she has for 21 years, bless her heart. Had it not been for her getting me to the hospital when I had that stroke I wouldn't be here today. So, I have a lot of 'thank-you-honeys' to be grateful for to her. And I want to be sure people know that.

"When I get calls for these benefit shows, I know that I'm not going to get paid. But the pay I get is seeing these beautiful little faces and to know that we're spending our time and money and appearing for free and that all proceeds are going to benefit these marvelous kids, where nobody loses. Everyone gets a gold medal. And that's important to me.

"And I also do some things for the Humane Society. I am a hopeless, there is no way you could cure me, animal lover. And I've done some benefits to open new shelters for unwanted pets. Of course, I want to take all of them home with me. I'd like to take them all home and turn 'em loose on a big ranch. Of course I can't do that, but if I can save the life of a little animal."

John Wilkinson performing with Barbara Dex.

CHAPTER 15

TCB Reunion

— 1 —

THE YEAR IS 2004. John continues to travel the United States and Europe, meeting with fans, performing for them, interacting with the various fan clubs, and telling his story to writers and filmmakers. Little did he know, this would be a historic year, the first time all five TCB Bandmates performed together on the same stage since the brief tour with the impersonator.

"All of us who worked with Elvis—and we were so close to each other 24/7—we became a family. After Elvis passed away, the guys in the TCB Band minus me, started to tour around and play in various and sundry places, and people were glad to see them. And the reason I couldn't join them is because of the stroke in 1989 that took away my ability to play guitar.

"I always liked the guys and we always got along real well. I'd hear about them playing overseas at big venues like Wembley, and my friend Peter Verbruggen, he formed a fan club in Belgium called 'Elvis Matters.' And he wanted to do something for his club members that would set his club apart as being the club for the fans, not for his pocketbook.

"He'd had me over to Belgium five or six times as I've explained, and the Belgians liked me. So finally, he decided to go for the coup de grace. First thing he did was get Joe Guercio, Elvis's conductor all those years, to come over. Joe never got the recognition he should have. Everybody likes and trusts Peter, with good reason. He's never given anyone reason not to trust him and he's earned the respect of the other guys.

"At dinner, he told me he was bringing Joe over to have him conduct the orchestra and let people get to know him. He pulled that off, the fans were real excited to see Joe. A lot of people really didn't know Joe. He was back there behind Ronnie and you couldn't hardly see him except every now and then his head would pop up."

Then Peter spilled the beans.

"*Now, I'm gonna try and do the really big thing and that is to reunite all five members of the TCB Band, all five of you on the stage at the same time. What do you think about that?*"

"*That would be something. The fans would really love to see that.*"

"*I'm gonna do it.*"

"He did. It took him a couple of years to work out all the things because of the boys' schedule and mine, and getting a place to perform. But he did, he got us all together. And it was set up for Oct 2 and 3, 2004.

"The TCB Band, consisting of Ronnie Tutt, Glen D. Hardin, James Burton and Jerry Sheff, were traveling with a singer called Jensen Bloomer, out of England, a very nice fella with a good voice. He doesn't dress like Elvis and he doesn't look like Elvis but he sings Elvis songs and he sings them very well."

John hadn't seen the guys in a long time but when he was in Belgium a year before the reunion, Peter and John happened to be in Brussels to pick up a friend and were at the Hilton sitting in the bar when they saw the guys come in, James, Jerry, Glen and Ronnie, checking in.

"They looked over and saw us and came over, all four of them.

"*John! Is that you?*"

"*Yeah, how you doing?*"

"Hadn't seen each other in years. All four of the guys came over gave me a hug and a handshake. It was wonderful. James Burton came over.

"*Man, I sure miss your rhythm guitar at my side.*"

"*Thank you, James I appreciate that!*"

"They had to check in as they were playing that night. Anyhow, they said they hoped we'd see each other again soon."

At that point, Peter gave John the details of his reunion plan.

"What they were gonna do is Peter advertised it as the TCB Band with Jensen Bloomer. Well, it sold out 10 weeks before the event took place, amazing. But what his idea was and I didn't know he was going to do this but was to have me as a special guest you know, to complete the five.

"At the start of the show, the TCB Band will come out and Jensen will do the first half of the show and sing his songs like he always does. Then the second half, Jensen will come out and do a couple of songs and then we'll announce:

"Notice the TCB Band only has four members up here? Well, there's a fifth one, you all know who he is, ladies and gentleman, say hello to John Wilkinson again."

"And I walked out and the place became unglued.

"Johnny, Johnny! Johnny!"

"Well, it put a chill up my back and Jensen handed me the microphone.

"Go get 'em!"

"And I did. And I hadn't rehearsed with the guys the songs I was going to do. But we didn't need to, we knew each other so well. I did 'Early Morning Rain,' 'Marie's the Name's Latest Flame,' among others.

"The audience reaction was great, they were standing up and cheering. I'd seen the kind of reaction they gave the other guys and I thought it was wonderful, they hadn't forgotten us. And they'd seen me before. But when I came out to be part of the guys, I took a tambourine with me, did my three songs and went off the stage and toward the end of the show, they had me come out again, and I stood next to James with the tambourine, and I kept up rhythm with Ronnie, and Jensen had me sing harmony with him on a couple of songs.

"It was incredible, just incredible.

"And after the show, Peter had us go upstairs to a balcony area and that's where he had the autograph tables set up for us to sign autographs, sell pictures, that kind of thing. The line went all the way around the rim of the upstairs and down the stairs and out the door! There were about 800 to a thousand people that wanted to shake hands with us and meet us.

"It was such a big event and I was so proud of Peter, and only Peter could have pulled this off because of the respect he commands in Europe. He's a journalist for Belgium's biggest paper and on a first-name basis with the crown prince of Belgium. He commands a lot of respect in that country and with good reason. He's a highly respected journalist and a highly respected person. After the show, the boys came to my dressing room, all of them.

"*God, John, they really went wild over you.*"

"*I've been here before.*"

"*Well, maybe we'll see if we can't do some more things with you. We could use more adoratrion and that kind of recognition!*"

"*I'd be glad to work with you guys again!*"

"So, a few weeks ago, I called James Burton.

"*There's a lot of promoters over there we're going to be working with and don't foreget John, we'd love to have you with us.*"

"*JB, call me. I'd love to do some things with you.*"

"So, they were serious about it and I get the feeling they really want me to come back and do what we did with Jensen in Belgium."

John reflected on his bandmates and what his relationship with them was like all those years touring with Elvis.

"James Burton of course played on all my records with RCA. In my mind's eye, there's not a better rockabilly player in the entire world. He can play everything from Chuck Berry to any country star, and he's played with all of them. He's a marvelous guitar player, ain't nobody better.

"Ronnie Tutt, definitely can hold a rhythm section together, ask Neil Diamond. That's who he works for now is Neil. And Ronnie's a fantastic person as well as being a very nice person. When we were in Belgium, Ronnie had his wife Donna with him and she came up to me.

"*John, how are you? You don't recognize me do you?*"

"*I know I've seen you before.*"

"I'm Donna Tutt."

"She was one of our flight attendants on our show plane for many years. She and Ronnie got married and had some kids. He's got 10 kids! They're beautiful kids. Ronnie's had some health problems, he had a heart attack. But she travels with him and gives him medication, that kind of thing.

"Jerry Scheff is a retired hippy. A wonderful guy, we've always been friends. Nobody plays the Fender bass or his signature bass like Jerry Scheff. He's got the most fantastic index finger on his right hand and is as quick as lightning. He wears a hearing aid now but he can still outplay any bass player I ever heard.

"Glen D. Hardin well, he was the group jokester and he still is. One of the funniest men I ever met in my life. He can play keyboards, piano, electronic, whatever you want, he can play with anybody. He's not a show-off like JLL but he can play with anybody. It was him and Guercio who wrote all the charts for all of Elvis's songs for the orchestra. He did all the orchestration charts with Guercio . Glen is a brilliant musician, for what we needed, for what Elvis needed, Glen was perfect. That's not saying a whole lot about Glen is it?

"When all of us were together on the plane or whatever, if it wasn't Jackie Kahane breaking us up it was Glen D. Glen D and JD Sumner and Jackie Kahane. Glen is funny as all get out. Wonderful human being. He's my drinking buddy. Terrific guy.

"Anything anyone ever said about us not getting along, that didn't happen. When those concerts happened it was magic. I wasn't playing guitar but what was magic is the guys were playing behind me. And the guys were great and the guys did everything I expected and it was a lot of fun. I got to introduce them on stage. It was a very happy reunion.

"James and I had a good relationship because James played on all my RCA records. So, to be reunited with James and having him back there playing, it was exciting. James and I had the opportunity, he came into my dressing room and we talked for a few minutes, and it was like old times. We never had a rivalry because there's no way I cold outplay James Burton, nobody can. But it was fun. We remembered some times we were playing together in rehearsals, just the two of us, figuring out what we were gonna play, and it was fun. We never had a rivalry. I love James, he's a terrific player, a nice guy and a good friend."

No doubt, fans should visit the fan Web sites of the various TCB Band members for updates on where and when they'll be playing next.

"The image is one thing and the human being is another ... it's very hard to live up to an image."
— Elvis Presley

DEDICATION

*A*ND THAT'S THE WAY IT WAS!

It's been one hell of a ride, rough in some places, smooth in others. But when it's all said and done I wouldn't trade a minute of the trip.

I want to dedicate this book to my parents, Virginia and the late Dr. Richard Wilkinson (6-30-1910 to 5-16-2005) without whose support, belief, understanding and genuine love I could never have attained the level of celebrity that I now enjoy.

To all of the musicians who have gone on to their rewards in heaven and those who are still among us, picking and grinning: My everlasting thanks for sharing all your neat tricks and licks with me.

I love you all. May all your dreams come true!

Made in United States
North Haven, CT
08 February 2025